THE FIRST EXPLORERS

John Vernon

B T Batsford Ltd London

AJ

First published 1978
© John Vernon 1978

ISBN 0 7134 0986 X

Printed by The Anchor Press, Tiptree, Essex
for the publishers B T Batsford Ltd
4 Fitzhardinge Street London W1H 0AH

Acknowledgment
The Author and Publishers thank the following for their
kind permission to reproduce copyright illustrations: the
Bodleian Library, Oxford, for figs 12, 15 and 26; the
Trustees of the British Museum for fig 5; the Mansell
Collection for figs 7 and 37; the Museu Nacional de Arte
Antiga, Lisboa, for fig 29; the Museum of the History
of Science, Oxford, for fig 36; the National Maritime
Museum for fig 46; the Radio Times Hulton Picture
Library for figs 20, 39, 40 and 45. The maps were drawn
by Chartwell Illustrators.

CONTENTS

INTRODUCTION

In the three volumes which form this series, the authors have traced out the exploration of the world from the time of the Vikings to that of Captain Scott. Each book deals with the work of six or more explorers. The first book covers the work of the earlier explorers down to Magellan; the second covers the work of early explorers who set out from Britain, down to Captain Cook; and the third investigates the work of those men who explored the interiors of the continents which had been discovered by the earlier adventurers. The history of exploration has failures as well as achievements, and the important lessons that were learned from the expeditions that failed are also demonstrated.

In considering the work of these explorers, the authors have shown how expeditions were planned, what dangers had to be overcome and what was finally achieved.

The work of British explorers was in part an effect and in part a cause of the emergence of Britain as a major world power. Certainly, the work of those people who explored the interiors of Canada, Australia, the USA and Africa provided British industrialists with new, larger markets and new sources of raw materials, which helped the industrial development of this country. We ought to know something about the work of the men who provided the opportunities for our countrymen to become more prosperous and so secured the base for the social and political developments which have led to the society in which we live today.

In each book contemporary illustrations and documents have been used — extracts from letters, diaries, or the explorers' own stories of their journeys. At the end of each chapter is a list of books recommended for those who wish to read further. Also at the end of each chapter is a variety of suggestions as to how a young reader, using his or her own imagination, can re-create the experiences of the individual explorers. Some of the questions in the 'Young Historian' sections may provide the basis for pupils looking for a subject on which they can base a project.

THE VIKINGS

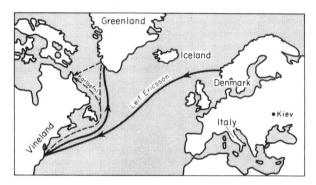

1   The voyage of Leif Ericsson.

2   The three major lines of the Viking expansion.

THE THREE-PRONGED BREAK-OUT

Until the year 793, the peoples of western and southern Europe had little contact with the people who lived in Norway, Sweden and Denmark (picture 1). By the year 1066, the people from these northern countries — Norsemen — had raided and looted, attacked and conquered, emigrated to and settled in so many countries and in such large numbers that this period, 793-1066, has been called the Age of the Vikings. In picture 2 you can see the main routes taken by the Norsemen. The Norwegians first went on a series of hops from island to island — from the Shetlands

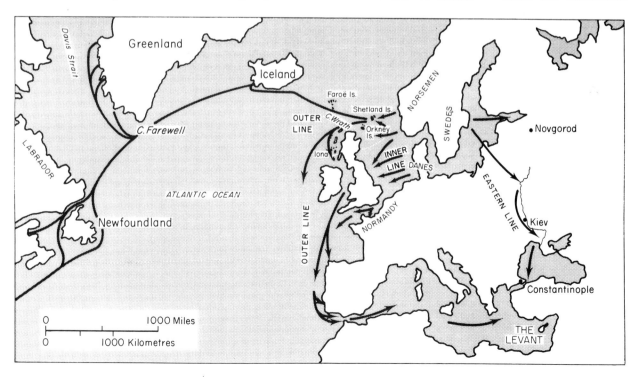

to the Faroes or the Orkneys. Then, as you can see, some went further west and settled in Iceland (874) where they built homes and lived as fishermen and dairy farmers. In 982, Erik the Red, an Icelander, was banished for three years for having slain a fellow-Icelander. He sailed to a land further west, which some Icelanders had discovered but not explored. He returned to Iceland in 985 and persuaded others to come to the new land, which he called Greenland. One of his followers, Erik Bjarni, lost his way and drifted to the south-west until he spotted a coastline. Because it did not look like the Greenland which Erik had described, Bjarni sailed away to the north-east until finally he came to Greenland. In 1003 Leif, Erik's son, decided to see Bjarni's new land for himself, and discovered the continent of America, which he christened Wineland

or Vineland (Picture 1) because of the fruits which grew in the warmer climate.

Other Norwegians took a southerly route via the Hebrides, along the coasts of Scotland, western England, Wales and Ireland, while some went on to northern France -- the Kingdom of the Northmen, later called Normandy. Others went on into the Mediterranean to found yet another great kingdom in Sicily.

So much for the Norwegians. If you look at picture 2 again, you will see that they took a route labelled the 'outer line'. The Danes took an 'inner line' route, along which some adventurers from southern Norway also sailed. It was these people who raided and plundered England, before they finally settled there and, under Canute, made it the centre of a great empire (page 12).

When the Swedes decided to break out, they took an eastern line (picture 3), establishing trading posts along the northern coast of what is now called Germany. Later, they took their

3   The Vikings into Russia.

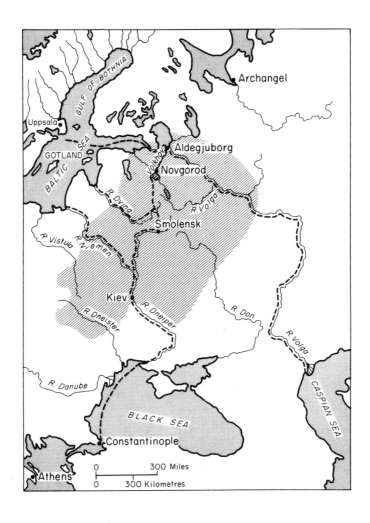

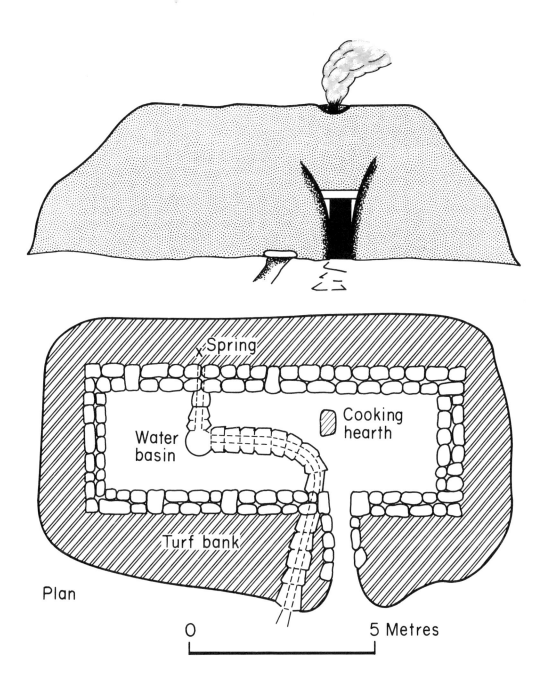

4   **The Viking hut.**

long boats along the mighty rivers through Russia and sold their furs and amber at Constantinople. Along the way, they set up trading posts and later established separate kingdoms or dukedoms at Novgorod, Smolensk and Kiev. The Slav natives of the vast area called the Swedes 'Rus' or foreigners. In time, the foreigners gave their name 'Rus' to the country — Russia.

Most of Denmark and Sweden was covered with forests, heath and marsh where no one could make a living. Norway was a mountainous country with a narrow coastal strip, scarred by the many rocky fjords or inlets. Life in these countries was very hard. People scraped a living as farmers, adding to their income and their diet by fishing. Some became traders, taking furs to foreign countries, leaving the

5

farming to their wives and younger children.

Almost everyone belonged to a clan led by a chief, who was the high priest as well as local ruler. The chief lived in a large house but the majority of the people lived in the long-room (picture 4), usually built of wood. In some places, local stone was used for the walls, timber being used only for the roof. Many houses had extra walls of peat, which was also used to make walls to keep animals out of the crop fields in the spring and summer, and to make sheds and pens for the animals.

A well-to-do farmer had a smithy for making tools and equipment, a bakehouse and bath-house, and separate long houses for the younger, married members of his family. Poorer farmers relied on their neighbours when they needed to repair tools or take a bath   in some villages a smith worked for all the local people.

Many farmers had slaves to help them clear forests, build houses and run the farms. In April, the ground was ploughed (picture 5) and crops of barley and oats sown, while the animals grazed in other fields on the new grass. Some peat was stored near the house to be used as fuel as well as a building material. In May and June, the villagers collected the eggs from the wildfowl and seagulls, helped in the lambing and shearing, and took the animals to the upland grazing areas — now cleared of snow. While the young people looked after the animals, the older men went on their overseas expeditions (page 7).

During July, August and September, hay was cut for winter fodder. Everyone collected as much fodder as possible, since this would decide how many animals could be kept alive during the winter and how many would have to be killed, their flesh being salted for eating during the long winter. In September and October, the barley and oats were harvested and the animals for whom there was no fodder were slaughtered. During the long winter the time was used for repairing and making tools, walls, and farm sheds for spinning and weaving the wool which, with the furs of wild animals and the leather from cattle, made the family's clothing.

In the winter months, there was plenty of time for sitting by the fire and for telling stories (which we now call 'sagas'), when children were told of their ancestors' exploits (picture 6). Our knowledge of the Norsemen is based largely on the translations of these stories, which were first written down in the twelfth century, long after the great days of the Norsemen were over. There was time during winter, too, for the Norsemen to reflect on the religious side of life and to worship Odin, the god of war, Thor, the god of the farmer and the owner of the thunderbolt hammer, and Frey, the god of love whose memory was recalled by the many weddings which were celebrated in the winter. These and minor gods lived in Valhalla where every Norseman hoped to join them when he died   preferably a hero's death.

The Norsemen had a local assembly (council) which they called 'Thing', where decisions were taken as regards emigration and where disputes between neighbours were settled. For example, a murderer was obliged to offer the family of the murdered person a money compensation. This might be refused and relatives of the dead man were entitled to seek violent revenge against the murderer or his family, in a system known as 'feud'.

5   The Vikings would have used a clumsy plough drawn by teams of oxen, such as this one which was found in medieval England.

WHY DID THEY BREAK OUT?

Here is an extract from a *Saga of the Men of Orkney*, which tells of the exploits of Svein Asleifsson, who lived around 1160:

> . . . Svein stayed at home in Gairsay all winter, and maintained 80 men at his own cost. He had a drinking hall so large that there was no other as large in the Orkneys. Svein would have great quantities of seed sown in spring and he would take a great share in this himself. But when this work was ended, he would go a-viking each spring, and would raid the Scottish Isles and Ireland, and he would come home at mid-summer. This he called 'spring viking'. Then he would stay home till the cornfields had been reaped . . . . Then he would go and not come back till one month of winter was over; this he called 'autumn viking'.

The term 'a-viking' is a Scandinavian word coming from *vik* (a creek, bay or fjord in which the sea-raiders used to lurk). Plundering gave Vikings a chance to add to their income. Their work at home left time for a-viking and the

6 An artist's impression of the Viking heroes. Others had a different idea of the barbarian hordes which attacked more civilized peoples.

stories that traders brought back told of the unguarded wealth of the rich south — abbeys and monasteries with gold and silver ornaments and unguarded farms with cattle and horses which could be slain and the dried and salted carcases brought back home.

Another explanation for the emergence of the Vikings was the pressure of a growing population in countries where land was scarce. Younger sons of chieftains who had no hope of inheriting land, and sons of yeoman farmers who did not look forward to being labourers, were among the Vikings who first created havoc in Europe and then learned to settle in the new-found lands.

HEROES OR VILLAINS?

From the 790s Europe was raided by plundering Vikings. The Anglo-Saxons feared the sight of Viking ships and later writers looked back with

horror to Viking attacks, as did the author of the twelfth-century Irish text, *The War of the Gaedhil with the Gaill* (Gaedhil = Irish; Gaill = Vikings) (picture 6).

> . . . if there were an hundred hard, steeled, heads on one neck, and an hundred sharp . . . brazen tongues in each head, and an hundred loud . . . voices from each tongue, they could not . . . tell what all the Gaedhil suffered, both men and women, laity and clergy, old and young, noble and ignoble, of hardship, and of injury . . . in every house, from these . . . wrathful . . . purely-pagan people.

In their own sagas, the Vikings always appear as heroic, hardy, strong, lovers of freedom and justice, fearless in battle and strong in friendship. We have to choose between these two accounts when we want to find out something about the Vikings. We can also rely on the work of the archaeologists, who have found several Viking ships as well as a good deal of jewellery, artwork, clothing and domestic utensils. In

1880, archaeologists unearthed the most famous example of a Viking ship at Gokstad, near Oslo in Norway (picture 7).

THEIR SHIPS

This ship was built about AD 900 and is typical of the longships. It is about 25 metres (80 feet) long from the prow to the stern. The keel was made from a single piece of oak. The hull, made from 16 'strakes' (planks), broadened out to about 5 metres (17 feet) amidships, where it was about 2 metres (6 feet) deep. Each strake overlapped the one below it and was riveted to it. All the grooves and joints were caulked with plugs of animal hair and wool woven in a loose cord.

Inside there were 19 ribs at 1-metre (3-feet) intervals on which were crossbeams to which the curving planks of the hull were nailed. Those below the waterline were lashed to the ribs by spruce roots, which allowed the ship to

7 An inside view of the Viking ship discovered at Gokstad, Norway, in 1880. The top two boards are reconstructions. Notice the way in which the mast is stepped into the keel, the deck boards, which were movable to allow for the bailing of water, and the holes through which the oars passed.

be supple enough to ride the heavy seas without breaking apart.

The ship did not have a fixed deck; the pine-wood floorboards only rested on the cross-beams and could be removed for extra storage. On each side you can see (picture 7) the holes for the 16 oars, each about 5 metres (16 feet) in length. The ship had one mast made of pine, about 30 centimetres (1 foot) in diameter and about 12 metres (40 feet) high. This mast was stepped into a heavy block of oak about 4 metres (12 feet) long, 60 centimetres (2 feet) wide and 40 centimetres (16 inches) thick, along the bottom of the ship. It was stepped so that it could be lowered by letting out the rope or wire which held the mast to the prow, but yet was firm enough against the force of the wind in the sail. The square-sail was made from coloured cloth woven in strips by the

8 A ship approaching land. This is redrawn from the Bayeux Tapestry, which tells the story of the Norman invasion of England in 1066. Notice the large sail, which was used only in a following wind, and the large rudder-paddle at the stern. Viking craft were like this.

women and serving girls. This sail was held in place by a series of ropes attached to the stern of the ship.

The rudder (picture 8) or steerboard (from which we get the term *starboard*), fixed at the stern, was a broad paddle, which went about 45 centimetres (18 inches) deep and was controlled by a tiller.

LIFE ON BOARD

Some ships were much larger than this: one has been found that is over 50 metres (160 feet) long. Others, merchant ships, were tubbier to allow for the carriage of more goods, and were also much higher out of the water.

The Gokstad ship would have had a crew of about 40 — oarsmen, steersmen and sail-controllers — and would have carried perhaps 30 others. There were lockers at the stern and in the prow to carry weapons, food and water; everything else was in the open air. Life was not very comfortable in these ships. When the ship sailed before the wind, shields were hung over the side to provide some extra space in the ship itself.

The men slept in sleeping bags made of leather or animal skins, although there were five collapsible bunks in the Gokstad ship. These may have been put up in the ship itself, or may have been put up in one of the three smaller dinghies which were pulled along behind

the larger ship. In good weather, it was possible to cook some barley gruel in an iron pot on the small hearth of flat stones. Normal food was a doughy flour, dried fish, butter and, perhaps, an onion, with water, buttermilk and beer to wash it down.

NAVIGATING FOR THE VIKINGS

The Vikings went a-viking in the summer months (page 7) when the winds were gentler, the seas calmer and the days both longer and warmer, without compasses or other instruments to help them. They relied on their own experience and the stories of other travellers. Here is one text which gives the instructions for anyone wishing to travel to Greenland (picture 2):

> From Hernar in Norway set sail due west for Hvarf in Greenland. . . . Sail to the north of Shetland . . . so that you can just sight it in clear weather; but to the south of the Faroes . . . so that the sea seems to be halfway up

the mountain; steer south of Iceland so that you can sight birds and whales from there.

THE RAIDERS

When the men went a-viking, they collected a fleet of 20 or 30 ships. Some wore chainmail shirts, the majority wore leather jerkins. Some were armed with a short bow and arrows, which could be used when approaching an enemy. Many carried the longspear and everyone had the longsword. The favourite weapon was the double-headed axe which required two hands to wield it. The leather shield, with its metal rim and boss, was used against arrows, spears and sword thrusts.

THE CHANGING PATTERN OF RAIDING

The story of the Danish attacks on England will serve as a model for the other attacks in Ireland, Scotland, Normandy, Sicily and Russia,

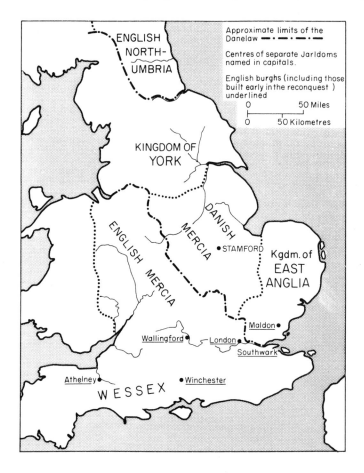

and even this account will have to be brief.

The first raiders got to the coast of England in 834 and attacked local abbeys and monasteries, terrorized local farmers (from whom they stole whatever they could carry off), and then returned home after a few weeks.

By 866 these raids had increased in number as well as in severity. Sometimes the raiders stayed in a fortified camp throughout the winter and resumed their plundering in the spring. In 866, Hingwar brought a large force. The weak, divided kingdoms of England (picture 9) offered little resistance and within two years Hingwar had ravaged the country from the English Channel to the River Clyde. He then turned to attack the kingdom of Wessex where, in 871, the 23 year-old Alfred had just become king. He has rightly earned the title of 'the Great' because of the way in which he led the people of his Anglo-Saxon kingdom first to resist the Danes, then to imitate them, and finally to defeat them. He built fortifications (or 'burghs') to withstand Danish attacks, built a fleet to keep the Danes away, and formed an army which — in 878 — defeated the Danish leader, Guthrum, at the battle of Eddington (near Chippenham). After his defeat, Guthrum agreed to become a Christian. Guthrum was allowed to remain as king of the Danish kingdom or Danelaw, while Alfred was recognized as the king of Wessex.

-------------------A THIRD STAGE-------------------

Having been at first mere raiders, then conquerors and settlers, the Danes now became 'natives' of their newly won country. They learned to live with the Anglo-Saxons, their children grew up in the Danelaw. They became more interested in farming. This helps us to understand why Alfred's son, Edward, and his grandson, Athelstan, were able to reconquer the Danelaw, and to beat off a combined attack from Ireland and Scotland in 937, so that by 954 the King of Wessex was ruler of all England.

--------- A SECOND DANISH INVASION---------

For 70 years after the death of Alfred, the Wessex monarchs ruled over England, allowing the people of the Danelaw to retain their own customs provided they acknowledged Wessex overlordship. All this came to an end in the reign of Ethelred the Unready (979-1016). He allowed the fleet to run down so that pirates once again found easy pickings along the south coast. This roused the interest of the Danes and Norwegians. In 991, King Olaf of Norway defeated the Essex army at the Battle of Maldon, the first defeat for a century. Ethelred tried to buy off the Danes with the payment of 10 000 pounds in silver. But this payment (or 'Danegeld') merely encouraged other invaders. In 994, Sweyn of Denmark came and collected 16 000 pounds. He returned in 1002 to get 24 000 pounds, after which the foolish Ethelred ordered the massacre of those Danes who lived in southern England, including Sweyn's sister. Sweyn came back again in 1007 to collect a Danegeld of 36 000 pounds and in 1010 he and Olaf of Norway combined to attack England. The *Saga of Olaf* tells of how they broke through the defences at London Bridge and made their way across England as far as the Severn:

> . . . when the host was ready they rowed up the river; as they came near the bridges they were shot at, and such large stones thrown down on them that neither their helmets nor shields could withstand them; and the ships themselves were greatly damaged and many retreated. But Olaf and the Northmen with him rowed up under the bridges, and tied ropes round the supporting posts, and rowed their ships downstream as hard as they could. The posts were dragged along the bottom until they were loosened from under the bridges. As an armed host stood thickly on the bridges . . . and the posts beneath were broken, the bridges fell with many of the men into the river; the others fled into the city, or into Southwark. After this they attacked Southwark, and captured it.

In 1011, Ethelred paid his last and greatest Danegeld, 48 000 pounds. Sweyn came in 1013 to conquer Wessex and set himself up as ruler of a united country. He died a few months after landing in England; his army chose his son Cnut (or Canute) as king. The death of the ineffective Ethelred and of his more able son Edmund Ironside (1013) left Wessex without a real king and in 1018 Cnut took a Danegeld of 82 000 pounds, which he used to pay off his army and set himself up as King of England. He was also, in 1018, King of Denmark and in

1028 became King of Norway. He much preferred the warmer climate of prosperous England to the bleakness of Denmark and Norway and so England became the centre of the Danish Empire. The Vikings had now ceased to be invading raiders and had become the ruling class in their new country.

_____THE END OF THE VIKING AGE_____

Cnut's decision to make England the centre of his large empire was only one of the signs that the days when men went a-viking were over. So many Scandinavians had left their home-lands that the spirit of enterprise and adventure seemed to have died. Those who had left were more concerned to found new kingdoms than with a-viking. There were Scandinavian kingdoms and dukedoms in Russia (picture 3), in Sicily and — from AD 1000 — in Normandy (picture 2) where the former raiders had created the most powerful dukedom in Europe. The conversion of the former raiders to Christianity, as in the case of Guthrum (page 11), was followed by the conversion of the peoples in the Scandinavian homelands. The peoples who had once fought against each other now turned in Christian unity to fight the Crusades against the Moslems, who had taken the Holy Places in Palestine. A new age had dawned.

THE YOUNG HISTORIAN

1 Make a large map of the world (which you will also require for later work) and mark on it the three routes taken by the Vikings.
2 Give a brief account of the seasons of the year as seen by a Viking family.
3 Make an illustration under the heading 'Viking food'.
4 Imagine that you are a young member of a Viking family. Tell the story of a raid as you might have seen it. Explain the preparation, the ships sailing away, and their return — some people have been lost at sea, others have come back with many 'presents'.
5 Write an account of a raid as it might have been told by (a) a Viking, (b) an English farmer.
6 Make a model of, or paint, 'Our Viking ship'.
7 As part of a class frieze on 'Exploration' paint, or draw, 'Our Viking chief with his armour'.
8 Draw or paint 'The raid on a Saxon village'.
9 What modern English words come from the names of the following Nordic gods: Tiu, Odin (or Woden), Thor, and Frey?
10 Find the names of five towns having the following Scandinavian endings: ay, ey, by, forth, thorpe, thwaite, toft, wick, with.

FURTHER HELP

Shorter information books
Donovan, F.R., *The Vikings* (Cassell)
Lobban, R.D., *The Vikings* (University of London Press)
Proctor, C.C., *The Vikings* (Longmans 'Then and There' series)
Reeves, M., *Alfred and the Danes* (Longman's 'Then and There' series)

Longer information books
Jones, Gwynn, *Scandinavian Myths and Legends* (Oxford University Press)
Simpson, J., *Everyday Life in the Viking Age* (Batsford)

Novels
Kipling, Rudyard, *Puck of Pook's Hill* (Macmillan)
Sutcliffe, Rosemary, *The Shield Ring* (Oxford University Press)
Treece, Henry, *Viking's Dawn* (Bodley Head)

Filmstrips
The Vikings (Visual Publications)
The Vikings: Life and Conquests (Rank)

THE TRAVELS OF MARCO POLO

VENICE IN THE THIRTEENTH CENTURY

Marco Polo was born in Venice in 1254, when it was the most important city-state in Europe, and the centre of the world's trade and commerce. It fully deserved the title 'the Queen of the Adriatic'. Its crowded wharves saw a continual flow of ships carrying goods from far-away places and in its busy squares the Venetians could see men from every country in Europe, Asia Minor and North Africa, babbling in unfamiliar tongues.

10 By the middle of the thirteenth century, there were well-defined trade routes to the East. The great 'Silk Road' ran across Central Asia; the longer sea route went south to Persia and India.

Venice was fortunate in that it was close to the heart of Europe and not too far, by sailing ship, from the eastern Mediterranean (picture 10). Goods from India, Persia, Arabia and China came by land to ports in the eastern Mediterranean, and so on to Venice. Goods from the Low Countries, England and Central Europe were brought by packhorse or by sailing ships travelling round the coast of Spain, and were shipped from Venice to the eastern Mediterranean.

Along the 'Silk Road' from the Far East there came silks, jewels, tea and porcelain, along with cloves from the Moluccas, pepper and ginger from Malacca, and cinnamon from Ceylon. Venetian merchants such as those portrayed by Shakespeare in *The Merchant of Venice*

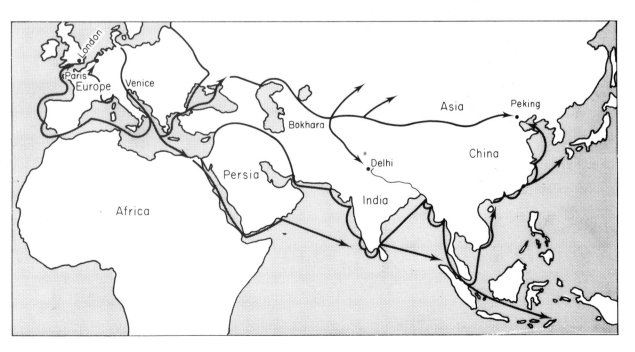

had become very rich from this international trade. Some provided the money to finance trade and commerce; others owned ships which sailed to every port in Europe or travelled along the long rivers of Russia (picture 3), carrying wool from England as well as spices from the Far East.

Venetians had founded commercial centres in Layas and Constantinople (pictures 3 and 13),

11 A medieval monk-artist's idea of the meeting between the Great Khan (on the left) and the Polo brothers, who were made to appear as monks in this monk's illustration.

and Venetian merchants were often away from home, looking after their business interests in these areas.

14

THE POLO FAMILY

Marco Polo's father, Nicolo, was a prosperous Venetian merchant with warehouses in Sudak in the Crimea. In 1260, Nicolo and his brother set out for Sudak. The journey was dangerous; some vessels were shipwrecked, others attacked by pirates, and a local war might interfere with their trade once they had reached their destination in the eastern Mediterranean.

In 1241, Genghis Khan had led a wave of invasions which had started in Mongolia and had ended with the conquest of the countries around the Baltic and the Danube (picture 3). In 1260, when the Polo brothers set out, Kublai was chosen as the Great Khan, ruler of all the local khans of the Mongol Empire. Kublai Khan was more interested in attacking the region to the south of Mongolia, and in 1279 he became the recognized ruler of China. Western European rulers soon realized how important the Khan was, and so they hoped to use him as an ally against the Moslems who controlled the Holy Places. In 1245, the Pope had sent ambass-

12 Marco Polo setting out on his famous voyage, together with his father and uncle. The French artist has shown the three travellers standing near the Grand Canal (just to the right of the centre bridge). Then they can be seen in a small boat (top right). Finally, they are shown aboard their galley (bottom), the sail of which catches a favourable wind (bottom right) and so takes them out to sea.

adors to make contact with the Great Khan, and King Louis of France also sent envoys to contact him.

The Polos found little trade being done in Sudak, perhaps because of a war somewhere along the 'Silk Road'. So they went with some Russian merchants to Sarai on the Volga, the capital of one of the local khans, to whom they sold their jewels at a great profit. They then found that yet another war prevented their travelling home. So they turned to the east and got to Bokhara (picture 10) on the eastern side of the Caspian Sea, where they stayed for three years (1265). They then met travellers from the court of the Khan of Persia, on their way to China, who invited the Polos to travel with them. They reached Peking after a year's journey, the first Europeans ever to have seen the capital of the empire ruled over by the Great Kublai Khan. He received them (picture 11) and allowed them to stay for a year in his court. He then sent them back as his personal ambassadors to the Pope, instructing them to ask the Pope to send out 100 priests to help in the conversion of the Chinese to Christianity. He also wanted the next visitors from the West to bring him some oil from the Church of the Holy Sepulchre in Jerusalem. To help them on their journey Kublai gave the Polos

a golden tablet on which was written:

By the strength of the eternal Heaven,
holy be the Khan's name.
Let him who pays him not reverence be killed.

This tablet was a sort of passport which enabled the Polos to get food, horses and lodgings as they made their way home through the Mongol Empire. Their journey back to Venice took them three years and when they finally got home in 1269 Nicolo found that his wife had died and Marco was now a fully grown 15 year-old.

MARCO POLO SETS OUT

While the elder Polos had been away, the old Pope had died and by 1271 no new Pope had been elected, so they were unable to carry out the mission on which they had been sent by Kublai. They decided to ask the advice of the Papal Legate at Acre, whom they had met in 1269. In 1271, they left Venice again, taking the 17 year-old Marco with them (picture 12). The journey to Acre took about six weeks. Here, they met the Papal Legate, Theobald, who told them to get the oil from Jerusalem, after which he would give them a letter to take to

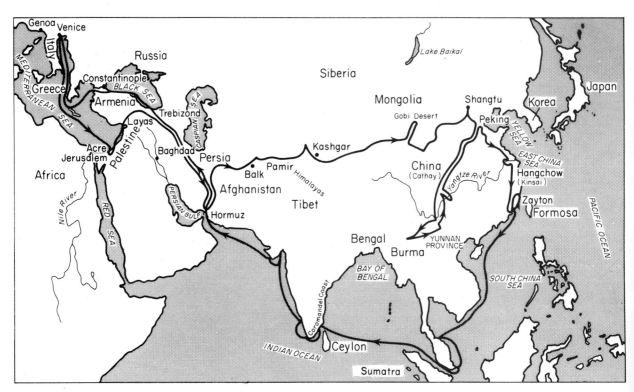

the Khan to explain why they were unable to bring the required number of priests with them. When they returned to Acre with the holy oil, they found that Theobald had been elected Pope and had taken the name Gregory X. He tried to help them recruit 100 priests, but unfortunately there were only two friars who were prepared to undertake the long and dangerous journey.

With the two friars they left Acre to make their way to Layas (picture 13), where they joined a caravan going to Persia. They carried with them the golden tablet-passport which they hoped would help them on their long journey. In picture 14 you will see how the goods were carried on camels; sometimes travellers used packhorses. In either case, the journey was bound to be slow and dusty. Marco Polo described the road they travelled along: there were cliffs to be scaled, ravines, streams and rivers to be forded, and wars to be avoided. In spite of the golden tablet, the two frightened friars decided to return, while the Polos journeyed on.

In Baku, Marco Polo saw his first oil well. He wrote: 'This oil is not good to eat; but it is

14   A camel caravan, probably carrying silk to or from Samarkan or Tashkent.

good for burning and as an ointment for men and camels affected with itch. Men come from a long way to fetch it.'

The Polos journeyed on via Baghdad, sometimes riding on mules or camels, sometimes riding in an uncomfortable cart, often walking and most nights sleeping out in the open. Baghdad must have been a welcome relief with its brightly tiled mosques and minarets, its groves of palm trees and its beautiful gardens. It is not surprising that Marco remembered it 'as the noblest and most extensive city to be found in this part of the world'.

Travelling about 30 kilometres (20 miles) each day, the dusty travellers made their way to the port of Hormuz (picture 13), where they hoped to find a ship to take them to China. Marco described the only ship that they were offered. The planks were held by wooden pins and by ropes of coconut husks. The ship had only one sail and no anchor, so that in rough weather it would be in danger of being driven ashore and wrecked. The Polos decided to make the long 200 miles back to Kerman where the road forked to the East.

13   A map showing the extensive travels of Marco Polo.

ACROSS THE ROOF OF THE WORLD

The first part of their journey lay through desert which, as Marco recalled, meant they had to carry all the food and water they might need for ten days until they came to the town of Balk. Here, they decided to take the more difficult of the three possible routes; they might have turned north to Samarkand, or south to Peshawar. Instead, they went east via Kashgar. This took them across the plateau of the high Pamir, as Marco Polo wrote: '. . . climbing so high that this is said to be the highest place in the world. There are quantities of wild sheep of huge size. No birds fly because of the height and the cold; because of this great cold, fire is not so bright here nor of the same colour as elsewhere and food does not cook so well.' Marco had noted a basic law of physics — that the boiling point of water varies with changes in the atmospheric pressure. High on the plateau, the atmospheric pressure was low and therefore their food was not being boiled at the correct temperature.

Having survived their journey across the roof of the world, they stayed for a while at Kashgar before setting out for the 30 days' march across the Gobi desert where, as Polo reported, there were many mirages to distract them. He also remarked that: 'It is a well-known fact that this desert is the abode of evil spirits, which lure travellers to their destruction. Losing the right path, and not knowing how to get back to it, they perish miserably of hunger.' The last town they saw before starting across this desert was Lop Nor, where the present-day Chinese government tests its nuclear weapons.

INTO CHINA

After the long journey through the Gobi desert, the Polos saw, once again, green fields and valleys, as well as villages and towns where they could get food and shelter. They entered China at the town of Kangchow, where they must have seen the Great Wall, although Marco does not mention this in his book.

From Kangchow they had a journey of 40 days to the Great Khan's summer residence at Shangtu. They were accompanied on their way by messengers from the Khan's court. Marco's account of this part of their journey described the exploits of the Mongol horsemen (the most agile mounted archers that Polo had ever seen). They could go ten days without taking a meal, lived off their horses' blood if necessary, and were a nomadic people who moved around seeking pastures for their flocks. They lived in felt-covered circular houses and their womenfolk did all the work — 'for the men do not bother themselves about anything but hunting and warfare and falconry'.

Polo also described the system of messenger posts which covered the Khan's empire. Along every major route there were a number of posts or forts, about 30 kilometres (20 miles) apart. Here the Khan's messengers could swap their horses for fresh ones and gallop on their way to the next post. Marco reckoned that there were 10 000 such posts where upwards of 300 000 horses were ready to do the Khan's work.

WITH KUBLAI KHAN

Marco and his father met Kublai Khan (picture 15) in his summer palace at Shangtu. Marco wrote about the marble palace, the bamboo pavilion, the gardens and woods, to such an effect that in 1816 the English poet Coleridge, having read Marco's book, sat down to write the famous poem *Kublai Khan*, which begins with the lines:

> In Xanadu did Kubla Khan
> A stately pleasure-dome decree

Marco described Kublai as 'of middle stature, his limbs well formed and in his whole feature there is just proportion. His complexion is fair and occasionally suffused with red, like the bright tint of the rose, which adds much grace to his countenance. He is the greatest Lord that is now in the world or has ever been.' Praise indeed from the son of one of the richest merchants in the richest city in Europe.

PEKING

Marco accompanied the Khan when he returned to his winter palace in Kanbalu, the modern Peking (picture 16). He described the city which was 10 kilometres (six miles) square, surrounded by a city wall 9 metres (30 feet) high and 9 metres thick, in which there were twelve gates each guarded by a thousand soldiers. Inside the wall, the streets were laid out in

15 An illustration from a French manuscript of 1400, showing the Polos presenting the Khan with a letter from the Pope.

straight lines — unlike the crooked, narrow alleys of European towns. It was, as Polo wrote, 'a chess board'. On the main streets were the great mansions of the rich, and outside the gates large hostels for foreign merchants. Marco wrote:

> To this city everything that is most rare and valuable in all parts of the world finds its way; and more especially does this apply to India, which furnishes precious stones, pearls and various drugs and spices. The quality of merchandise sold there exceeds also the traffic of any other place; for no fewer than a thousand carriages and packhorses loaded with raw silk make their daily entry; and gold tissues and silks of various kinds are manufactured to an enormous extent.

Polo describes the Khan's palace with its golden tiles, where 6000 guests sat down to a meal on special occasions, such as the Khan's birthday. Here, too, was the royal mint where the Khan appeared, to Marco, to have performed a miracle by producing paper money:

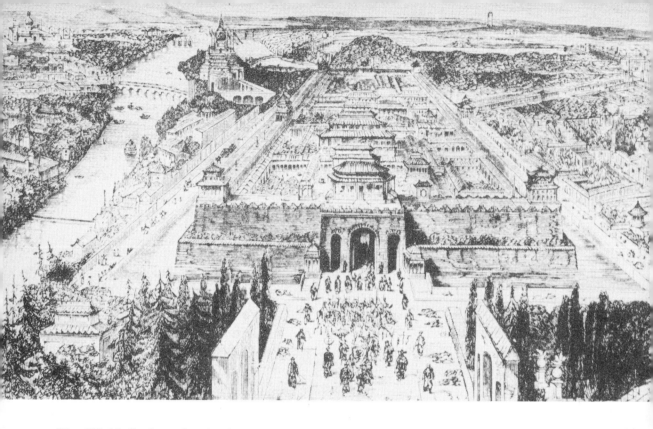

He [Kublai] has the bark stripped from mulberry trees . . . and takes from it that thin layer that lies between the coarser bark and the wood of the tree. This being steeped, and afterward pounded . . . until reduced to pulp, is made into paper, resembling that which is made from cotton. . . . He has it cut into pieces of different sizes, nearly square, but somewhat longer than they are wide . . . . To each note a number of officers . . . not only subscribe their names but also affix their seals . . . the principal officer, having dipped into vermilion the royal seal, stamps the piece of paper . . . . Counterfeiting it is punished as a capital offence.

GOVERNOR POLO

The Khan admired the young Marco and appointed him to the royal service. He sent him to Yunnan, which was a four-month journey, and Kinsai (modern Hangchow — picture 17), the port where Polo saw thousands of junks laden with tons of pepper, spices, ebony, jewels and silk. This trade — exceeding even that of Venice — had enriched thousands of merchants, who occupied huge houses with large gardens

16   The Tartar Palace in Peking, China.

and who lived a highly civilized life with their printed books (many centuries before Europe had printing presses), and beautifully prepared and exotic food. In between journeys for the Khan to Burma, Tibet and other outlying provinces, Marco served for three and a half years as governor of Yangchow. He was also a frequent visitor to the Khan's capital, crossing the great bridge across the river 16 kilometres (ten miles) from Peking. This, he recorded, was 300 paces long and wide enough to allow ten horsemen to ride side by side. It had 24 arches and 24 piers in the water and was made of the finest grey marble, with its elaborate columns decorated by carvings of animals. All this when London had a small, wooden bridge.

Marco also visited India, Java, Sumatra and other islands with which China traded, and by the time he told the Khan that he wished to return to Europe, he had seen sights which no Westerner had ever seen. In 1292, he set out on his long journey home. As you can see from the map (picture 18) he made the journey by sea as far as Hormuz. Along the way, he again saw wonderful sights, such as the pearl fishers at work in Ceylon.

VENICE AGAIN

The journey back to Venice took three years. When the party arrived there in 1295, they had been away for 24 years and none of their relatives or friends recognized them with their Chinese-style clothing. Their problem was made greater because after being away for so long they had forgotten how to speak Italian. Marco had learned at least four new languages, but the Venetians could not understand any of them.

17 A fourteenth-century view of Kinsai. On the far shore, you can see some of the magnificent houses. On the river, rich people are taken on a pleasure trip.

When at last they managed to make themselves understood and told of the wonderful things they had seen, they were mocked — as madmen! But the business-like Venetians understood, and believed, the value of the jewellery which the Polos had sewn up in their clothing.

THE BOOK

In 1295, the year of the return of the Polos, Venice and Genoa went to war. Marco, now 41 years old, was captured by a Genoese fleet when he was sailing with a fleet of 15 galleys towards Constantinople. He was imprisoned

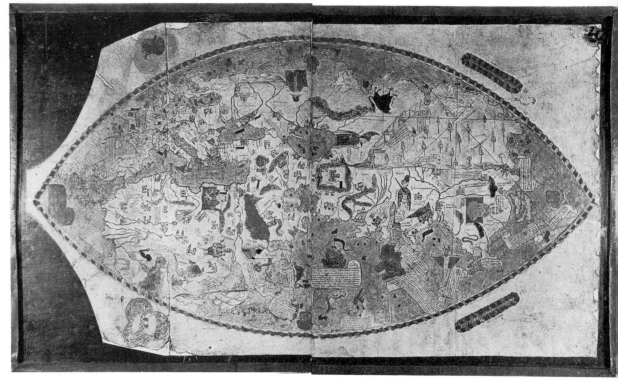

18   This map was painted in 1457. It shows Europe on the left and China on the right. Columbus's discovery of the land mass of America did not take place until 1492. After that, all maps had to be redrawn.

in Genoa where he told his fellow-prisoners about his experiences in the Far East. One of the prisoners was named Rustichello. He had been an author of romantic stories about King Arthur and his Knights. He persuaded Marco to allow him to write down the story of the journeys. It took until 1299 to finish writing the story. In that year Venice and Genoa made a peace treaty and the prisoners were released. Because Europe was more backward than China, Polo's book was not printed until 1477. However, the story of Marco's journey became known to many merchants and travellers, and for about 50 years many travellers and traders followed in Marco's footsteps. Then in 1371, the Chinese rose in rebellion against their rule by the Mongols and drove them out, closed the frontiers of their country to foreigners, expelled foreign traders and so prevented anyone bene-fiting from journeying along the 'Silk Road' for trade with China. At about the same time, the Turks began to make the journey along that same route — which was even less safe than it had been in Marco's time — so that from about

1375 onwards there was almost no trade be-tween East and West.

THE LASTING EFFECTS

So, at first sight, Marco's experiences may seem to have had no lasting effect. However, after 1477 printed copies of his book began to appear. His stories about the wealth of China and other countries aroused the interest of people at the end of the fifteenth century. One person whose interest in exploration was stimulated by Polo's book was Christopher Columbus. So there is a link between the long journey of Marco Polo and the work of a later, perhaps greater, explorer, Columbus (pages 47-59). He would have studied maps drawn by cartographers relying on the stories of travellers such as Polo. As you can see from picture 18, while they knew that the world was round, they did not know about the land mass in the West — America. They did know about the East and they hoped that there might be an easy way to that fabulously wealthy region if they sailed towards the West, going around the world until they hit the Chinese mainland, and so made their way to the spices and other valuable products of the Indies.

THE YOUNG HISTORIAN

1 On your map of the world mark:
  (a) the 'Silk Road' (picture 10), and
  (b) the routes followed by Marco Polo (picture 13).
2 Imagine that you are Marco Polo visiting the harbour of Venice to see if there is any news about your father. Give an account of your visit. (Picture 12 might be of some help; but you will find pages 13-14 useful.)
3 Write the letters which might have been written by:
  (a) A traveller making his way by sea to Constantinople (see picture 12 for the ships). What dangers might he have met? Why was he travelling?
  (b) The Khan who wanted the Pope to send priests to China.
4 Find out more about the careers of (a) Genghis Khan, and (b) Kublai Khan.
5 Write the letter which Nicolo Polo might have written to explain his long absence from home and describing his meeting with the Khan (pictures 11 and 15).
6 Write an extract which might have appeared in the diary of a traveller who followed the same route as Marco Polo. If you choose carefully the particular experience you write about, it ought to be possible to compile a collection of extracts with other members of your class and so produce a folder or diary.
7 Imagine that you are a merchant from Kinsai who has travelled to Venice (picture 12). Write the account you might have given of your opinion of Venice, known as the 'Queen of the Adriatic'.
8 Write the headlines which might have appeared in:
  (a) Chinese newspapers reporting the arrival of Marco at the Khan's court;
  (b) Venetian newspapers reporting the stories told by Marco on his return home;
  (c) Chinese papers reporting the imprisonment of Marco Polo.
9 Paint or draw an illustration to go with any part of Marco's experiences. As in Question 6, a selection of what you wish to illustrate could enable you to make a class folder.
10 Make up your own plays on:
  (a) How the Polos were treated by a Mongol innkeeper (i) before, and (ii) after he had realized that they had the Khan's golden tablet;
  (b) How the Polos were received when they returned home;
  (c) Polo telling his story in the Genoese prison.

FURTHER HELP

Books
Collins, R., *East to Cathay* (World's Work)
Collis, Maurice, *Marco Polo* (Faber)
Polo, Marco, *The Travels* translated by R. Latham (Penguin Classics)
Rugoff, M., *Marco Polo's Adventures in China* (Cassell Caravel)

Filmstrips
Great Explorers: the Travels of Marco Polo (Visual Publications)
Marco Polo (Ladybird)

AROUND THE AFRICAN CAPE WITH DIAZ

EASTERN TRADE

The Chinese had closed their frontiers to foreigners and the old 'Silk Road' was not as crowded as it had been in Marco Polo's time. But there was still a flourishing Far Eastern-European trade involving, in particular, the Spice Islands, which today are called the Moluccas and are situated to the east of Borneo and to the south of the Philippines (picture 53).

19 A map showing how the Ottoman Empire had spread into Europe, cutting across the medieval trade routes to the East (pictures 10 and 13). Europeans had to find another route to the fabled wealth of Cathay.

So Venice and Genoa continued to thrive as centres through which passed the merchants and traders of central and northern Europe, who sent their goods along the Mediterranean to ports at its eastern end. From here, these goods were taken by packhorse or camel (picture 14) to the markets of the Far East, where they were exchanged for the valuable spices.

But in 1453 this route was closed when the Turks captured Constantinople. You can see from the map (picture 19) how large the Turkish (or Ottoman) Empire was, and you can also see how the presence of that empire proved an obstacle to the old trade routes to the Far East. We will see in the next four chapters how people tried to get over this difficulty.

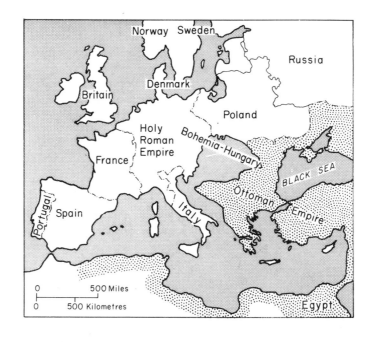

Text in image: PRINCE HENRY OF PORTUGALL

HONI · SOIT · QVI · MAL · Y · PENSE

CEVTA

20   Prince Henry of Portugal, known as the Navigator (1394-1463).

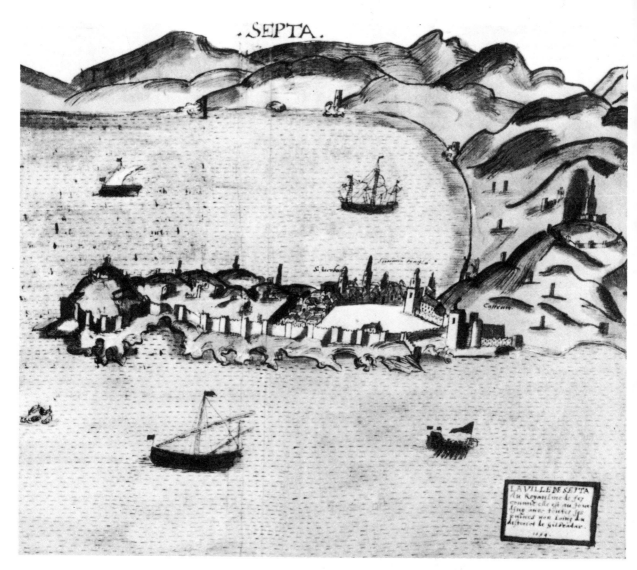

.SEPTA.

LA VILLE DE SEPTA

SPICES

Today, we expect our butchers to provide us with fresh meat all the year round. However, until the eighteenth century, there was little winter fodder on which to feed animals, so that each autumn there was a great slaughter of all except a few special animals (page 6). The meat — beef, pork, mutton — was dried and preserved for consumption during the winter. Also, we expect our butchers and greengrocers to have refrigerated stores. Many of us have our own domestic refrigerators and freezers. But until the late nineteenth century, there was no such luxury. Food was either eaten when it was fresh (in the spring and summer) or was taken from stores where it was kept through-

21 The port of Ceuta was captured by Prince Henry during his struggle against the Moors. This painting appeared in a French atlas of 1594.

out the long winter.

We have to understand this food problem — which was partly a problem of storage — before we can understand why people in the fifteenth and subsequent centuries bought so much spice, such as pepper, cloves and cinnamon. These were used not merely to add a taste to the food, as they are today. They were required

22 A caravel with its various sails which enabled the captain to sail his boat into the wind. This was an advance on the techniques known to the Vikings (picture 8).

26

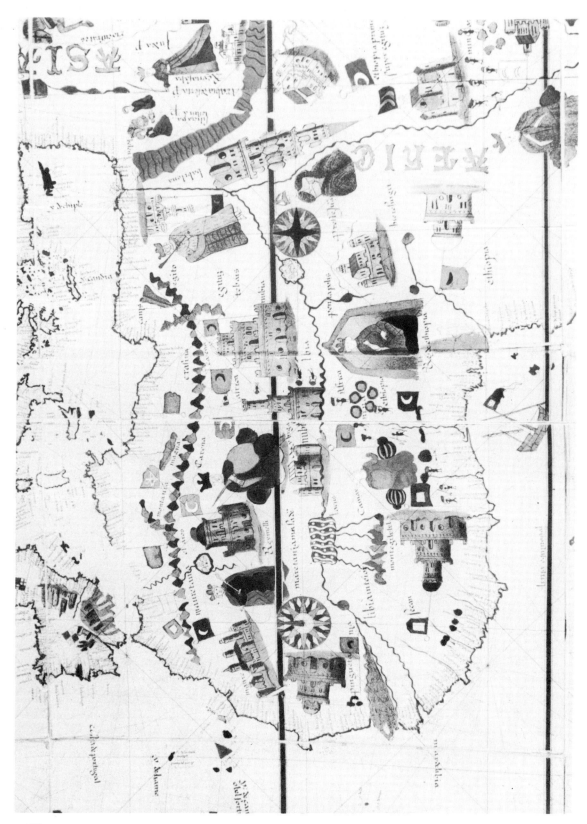

28

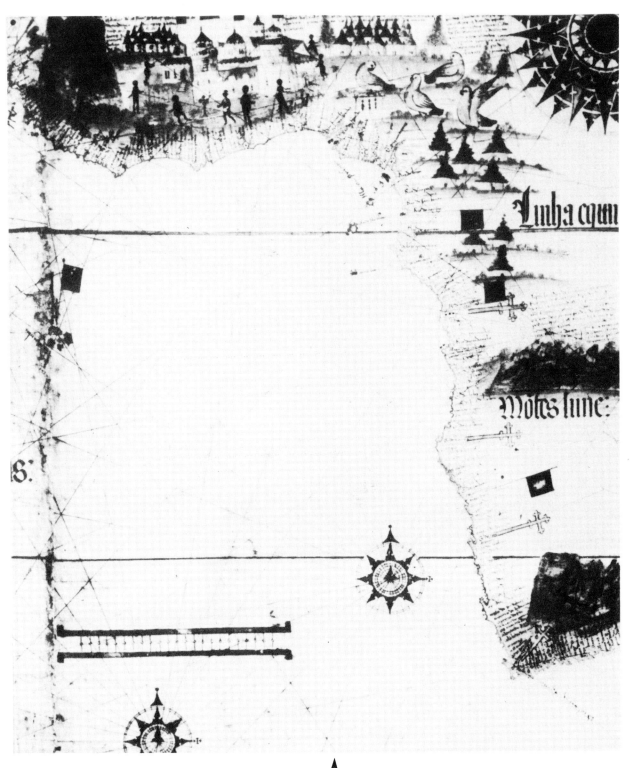

Linba cqui

Motes lune:

S.

This map of Africa was drawn by Juan de la Cosa, who became chart-maker to Columbus. Prester John's kingdom is by the right-hand compass mark, and the River Niger is shown as joining the River Nile.

24 A map of the west coast of Africa published in 1502, on which the map-maker has named some of the great cities which it was believed lay on that great continent. The large crosses on the mainland mark the furthest points reached by different voyagers.

to disguise the fact that the meat, fruit, butter or whatever, was rotten. By using heavy doses of spices the people hoped to deceive their taste-buds. They could not, of course, deceive their stomachs, and the frequent deaths from dysentery, vomiting and other stomach disorders were proof of the poor quality of the food consumed.

This explains the heavy demand for spices and the high prices which merchants charged and customers paid. A trader could buy 50 kilograms of cloves for only 4 ducats in the Moluccas and sell them for 400 ducats in the European markets. This meant that, after paying off the expenses of a trip, a merchant could expect to make a huge profit from the sale of spices.

This also explains why so many people were eager to find a new route to the valuable Spice Islands.

HENRY THE NAVIGATOR
(1394-1463)

Henry was the third son of King John of Portugal (1385-1433). When Prince Henry was 21 he had fought against the Moslem Moors at the siege of Ceuta on the coast of North Africa (picture 25). At that time, the Sahara was a valuable trading centre and Henry hoped that Portugal might become rich if only it could capture the bulk of the trade in gold, ivory, pepper and slaves. But he realized that Portugal was too weak to do this on its own, because the Moors were too strong.

This led him to consider the possibility of sending Portuguese sailors and soldiers around Africa to link up with the mythical Christian, Prester John, who was believed to have founded a Christian kingdom in the region we now call Abyssinia (picture 23). This king, it was thought, could put an army of a million Christian soldiers into the field, drawn from the 72 kingdoms he was supposed to control. In reality, there was no such king or empire; but the fact is that Henry and others believed there was, and one of the main reasons for Portuguese exploration along the coast of Africa was to make this hoped-for link which would have enabled the Portuguese, aided by Prester John, to defeat the Moors.

25 A map which shows the slow progress made by the Portuguese in their exploration of the coast of Africa.

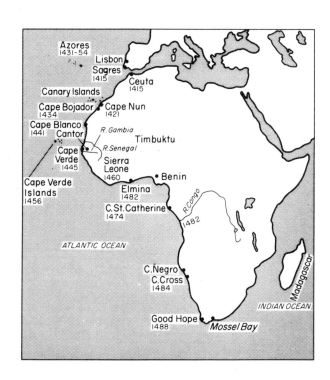

If you look at picture 18 you will see that while people by then believed that the world was round, they did not believe that there was a route round the tip of Africa. Henry's main task was to help Portuguese sailors find a way round this vast continent. A medieval chronicler wrote about Henry:

After the taking of Ceuta in 1415, he always kept ships well armed against the Infidel both for war, and because he had a wish to know about the land that lay beyond . . . the Cape called Bojador [picture 25]; up to this time . . . the nature of the land beyond that cape was not known with any certainty. . . . He sent his own ships to these countries in order to acquire knowledge in the service of God, and of the King Edward, his brother . . . . And this was the first reason for his enterprise.

And the second was the thought that if in these territories there should be any . . . Christians, or any harbours where men could enter they could bring to the realm many goods at little cost; . . . and that one could carry to these regions the merchandise of our realm, the sale of which would be of great profit to the natives.

The third reason was this: that it was said that the power of the Moors in this land of Africa was very great . . . and the Prince sent his people in quest of information, in order to know the full extent of the Infidels' power.

The fourth reason was this: . . . the Prince had never found a Christian king . . . outside this kingdom who . . . was willing to aid him in this war. He desired to know whether in those regions there might be any Christian princes in whom the love of Christ was strong enough to cause them to aid him against these enemies of the faith.

_____ A SCHOOL OF NAVIGATION _____

In 1419, Henry moved his own headquarters to Sagrès (picture 25) on the southernmost tip of Portugal. By 1437 he had built a school of navigation on this rocky outpost where he collected a team of sailors, navigators, mapmakers and astronomers who, between them, built up a body of knowledge about ships, navigation, instruments and the use of stars to help determine position and direction. He also encouraged the building of new ships,

called caravels (picture 22) in which, he hoped, his countrymen would find their way round the Dark Continent of Africa.

These ships were small — about 30 metres (100 feet) in length and about 6 metres (20 feet) broad, with 'castles' at either end. There were three, sometimes four, masts. In addition to the traditional square-sails, the main mast carried an extra small one, known as the top-sail. There were also two other new sails: a triangular fore-and-aft 'lateen' sail on the stern (or mizzen) mast, and a square spritsail under the bowsprit. These sails enabled the ships to sail closer to the wind. For example, if a captain wished to sail westwards into a westerly wind, he could first sail north-west for a certain distance and then 'tack' through an angle of 90 degrees so that he was sailing south-west. A series of such tacks would enable the ship to make progress even against unfavourable winds.

The crew lived under the forecastle in dark, damp and rat-infested conditions, stifling in the summer and bitterly cold in the winter. The sort of food carried in these ships may well have been like that taken aboard the East Anglian herring-fishing ship in 1615:

Beere. A gallon of beer a day.
Bisket. 1lb a day.
Oatmeale or Peaze. 1 gallon a day.
Bacon. '2 pounds of bacon for 4 meales in a weeke.'
Fresh Fish. 'They may take, daily, out of the sea, as much fresh fish as they can eate.'
Butter. 'To allow every man and boy a quarter of a pound of butter a day.'
Cheese. ½ lb of Holland cheese a day.
Vinegar. 3 pints a day among 16 people.
The following stores were also taken: Aquavita, 4 gallons; Zantoyle, 2 gallons; Honny, 2 gallons; Sugar, 4 lb; Nutmegge, ¼ lb; Ginger, ½ lb; Pepper, 1 lb.

This food was supposed to be enough for a trip of sixteen weeks. If you remember that the Portuguese were often away for much longer periods, you will understand that this food soon became soggy and maggoty, the water became stale, the beer went flat and the wine went sour. It is not surprising that over half a crew could be expected to die during a long voyage and that a whole crew might be affected by scurvy.

Navigational instruments were very simple and inaccurate. There was a compass mounted on a card, but no one then understood the difference between the Magnetic North (to which the needle pointed) and the true North. The height of a star, usually the Pole Star when at its zenith, was observed by an astrolabe or a cross staff. Using these star measurements and a book of tables, a captain could work out the latitude in which he was sailing. But there was no accurate way of calculating the longitude; therefore a captain had to estimate his position by assessing his ship's speed over a certain length of time (the method known as 'dead reckoning').

ON THEIR WAY

So, in small ships, eating poor food, not being fully aware of their position and sailing into the unknown, the Portuguese, inspired by Prince Henry, sailed along the coast of Africa. If you look at picture 25 you will see the slow progress they made from 1432 to that great day when Diaz finally got round the Cape in 1488. If you look at picture 24 you will see a copy of a map which was published in 1502; the mapmaker has shown, by crosses, the furthest points reached by different travellers and has also tried to show some of the great cities of the African kingdoms.

The first major obstacle proved to be Cape Bojador (picture 25). One sailor wrote:

. . . at last after twelve years of effort, the Prince has a barque fitted out, appointing as the captain his squire, Gil Eannes, whom he afterwards knighted and rewarded largely . . . on this voyage, regardless of all peril he passed beyond the Cape, where he found . . . lands without houses, but saw the footprints of men and camels. . .

Another major step was taken when Cadamosto sailed 400 miles beyond Cape Bianco until he reached the Senegal River (picture 25). He sailed 200 miles along the river and wrote this account of his journey and of the king of the region:

This king is lord of a very poor people, and has no city in his country, but villages with huts of straw only . . . he has no regular income. Each year the lords of the country present him with horses (which are esteemed owing to their scarcity), forage, cows and goats, vegetables, millet and the like. The

King supports himself by raids which result in many slaves from his own as well as neighbouring countries. He employs these slaves in cultivating the land . . . but he also sells many in return for horses and other goods.

These people . . . constantly go naked, except for goatskins fashioned in the form of drawers. But the chiefs and those of standing wear a cotton garment. They have no ships; nor had they seen any from the beginning of the world until they saw those of the Portuguese.

THE GAMBIA RIVER

Diego Gomes set out after hearing Cadamosto's report. He wrote:

After passing a great river beyond Rio Grande, we met such strong currents in the sea that no anchor would hold. The other captains . . . begged me to turn back. As the current grew even stronger we put back and came to a land, where there were groves of palms near the shore with their branches broken. . . . We went back to the ships, and next day made our way from Cape Verde and saw the broad mouth of a great river, which we entered and guessed to be the Gambia. We went up the river as far as Cantor. Farther than this the ships could not go, because of the thick growth of trees and underwood. When the news spread through the country that the Christians were in Cantor, people came from Timbuktu in the North, from Mount Gelu in the South to see us . . . . I asked the natives of Cantor about the road to the gold country. They told me the King lived in Kukia and was lord of all the mines on the right side of the river of Cantor, and that he had before the door of his palace a mass of gold . . . so large that twenty men could hardly move it . . . . While I was thus trading with these negroes, my men became worn out with the heat, and so we returned towards the ocean.

FORT ELMINA

Gomes returned home in 1458. Prince Henry died in 1460, his dream of finding a route round Africa still unfulfilled. But the work went on. Fernao Gomes, a merchant from Lisbon, paid the King to allow him to have total control of trade with West Africa. In return he promised that his seamen would explore a new section of the coast each year. It was Fernao Gomes's men who first discovered that the coast of Africa curved to the east before carrying on southwards again. Their work included the discovery of the valuable Gold Coast (now Ghana). King John II (1481-95) took control of the work of exploration as well as of trade with Africa. He had a fort built at Elmina (picture 26), as a contemporary writer noted:

. . . he ordered the equipping of a fleet of ten caravels and two urcas [hulks] to carry hewed stones, tiles and wood, as well as

munitions and provisions for six hundred men, one hundred of whom were craftsmen and five hundred soldiers . . . . The work progressed so rapidly that in 20 days the outer wall of the castle was raised to a good height, and the tower to the first floor.

PRESTER JOHN ALIVE?

The building of Fort Elmina allowed the Portuguese to develop a valuable trade with the tribes along the coast of West Africa. In particular, there was a valuable trade in gold. It was during the reign of King John II that the hopes of getting round Africa were raised to new heights. Not only had Portuguese sailors gone a vast distance along the African coast (picture 25) but they also picked up reports of the existence of a Christian kingdom in the interior

26 Fort Elmina from the sea. The Portuguese built this and other forts along the coast of Africa as places where their sailors could rest and their merchants establish their businesses.

33

or on the eastern coast. As one writer noted at the time:

Among the many things which King John learnt from the ambassador of the King of Benin . . . was that to the East of Benin . . . lived the most powerful monarch of these parts, who was called Ogane . . . the King and his cosmographers, . . . concluded that he must be Prester John. It also appeared to King John that if his ships continued along the coast they had discovered, they could not fail to reach the land . . . . Therefore taking into consideration all these

27 In this sixteenth-century watercolour, Portuguese seamen are shown rowing away from their shipwrecked vessel, whose mast can be seen in the background.

facts which increased his ardour for the plan of discovering India, he determined to send immediately in the year 1486 both ships by sea and men by land, in order to get to the root of this matter . . .

———————— AROUND THE CAPE ————————

In 1487 Bartholomew Diaz set out with three caravels to make yet another journey of exploration along the western coast of Southern Africa. It is well to recall the hazardous nature of the Portuguese exploration in these small ships (page 31). Diaz experienced one of the common hazards facing men who ventured far away from

28 This is an extract from the Catalan Map drawn in 1375. It shows an Arab merchant approaching King Mansa Musa, who is holding a large nugget of gold in his hand.

Portugal when his ship was caught in a gale which blew for almost a week and which drove him out to sea. Many ships had been wrecked in such gales (picture 27); Diaz and his men were more fortunate. After thirteen days, they sailed back eastwards again, hoping to find the coast of Africa. In fact, he failed to find a coast as he had expected. He continued to sail further east until his men forced him to turn to the north. He then came to the coast, only to find that the land was running away in an east-to-west direction and not, as is the case along the western coast, in a north-to-south direction. Diaz had in fact sailed round the Cape without knowing it.

He landed at Mossel Bay (picture 25) to get some water and food. He then took his ship even further to the east until he found that the land was curving away to the north again. His men now forced him to retrace his route. They had been away from home for too long; their food supply was running out; and what unknown dangers awaited them in this new ocean? The way back, however, was almost as unpleasant as the last days they had spent

along the western coast of Africa. There was a fierce gale, which led Diaz to report to the King that he had found the Cape of Storms. The King welcomed him back to Lisbon and declared that the name of the new cape should be 'Good Hope'.

One of those who wrote about Diaz's exploration was Christopher Columbus. On his copy of *Imago Mundi*, a geography book, he wrote:

In December of this year, 1486 [Columbus was wrong about the date which should be 1488], there landed at Lisbon Bartholomew Diaz, whom the King had sent to Guinea to explore the land and who reported that he had sailed 600 leagues [1650 kilometres (1050 miles)] beyond the furthest point reached hitherto, that is 450 leagues to the South and then 150 leagues to the North, as far as the Cape of Good Hope, its latitude, as determined by the astrolabe, being 45° South . . . and its distance from Lisbon 3100 leagues. This voyage he had depicted and described from league to league upon a chart, so that he might show it to the king; at all of which I was present.

The Portuguese had found a route to the fabulous wealth of the Spice Islands after over 60 years of exploring along the African coast.

THE YOUNG HISTORIAN

1 On your map of the world mark the route taken by Diaz.
2 Write the headlines which might have appeared in:
(a) A Venetian newspaper above the report of the loss of Constantinople, 1453 (you might also write a brief report of the effect of this loss);
(b) A Lisbon newspaper after the reporter had visited Sagrès (page 31);
(c) A Lisbon newspaper on the completion of Fort Elmina (picture 26);
(d) A Genoese newspaper above the report of Diaz's success.
3 Imagine that you have come on a time-machine from the fifteenth century to today. Write an account of your impressions of the quantity, quality and variety of food available today.
4 Write the obituary which might have appeared about Prince Henry (pictures 20, 21 and 22). Briefly summarize the motives which drove him to an interest in exploration.
5 Write the letter which might have been sent by a sailor after three weeks at sea (picture 22, and the information on food on page 31).

6 Make a time chart in which you show the slow progress made by the Portuguese along the coast of Africa (pictures 24 and 25). How do you account for the slow progress?
7 Write the letter which might have been sent by one of Diaz's sailors after his return home in 1486.
8 Make an illustration entitled: (a) our food (page 31); (b) our caravel (picture 22).
9 Make up a short play on: (a) Diaz's argument with his men who want to return home; (b) Portuguese welcome to the returning hero.

FURTHER HELP

Books
Hale, J.R., *Age - of Exploration* (Time Life)
Hobley, L.F., *Early Explorers* (Methuen)
Plunket, I.L., *The Story of Henry the Navigator* (Lutterworth Press)
Sterling, T., *Exploring Africa* (Cassell Caravel)

Filmstrip
Seawards to India (Visual Publications)

TO INDIA WITH VASCO DA GAMA

THE DIVIDED WORLD, 1494

Diaz had shown that it was possible to sail round the Cape of Good Hope. It was only a question of time before someone had the courage to sail along the eastern coast of Africa and then take the last stage of the journey across the ocean to India. In 1492 Columbus had shocked the world by sailing to the west where he had discovered, as he thought, a westerly route to the Spice Islands. Columbus (pages 47-59) had sailed on behalf of the newly united kingdom of Spain and many people thought that there was a danger of a trade-exploring war between Spain and Portugal. This would have been disastrous for Christian Europe, which wanted as much unity as possible between the Christian powers in order to meet the threat offered by the Turks (picture 19) and the Moors.

In 1494, the Pope intervened to try and ward off this danger of war. He drew a line on a map of the world and declared that Spain had the sole right of exploration and conquest of all lands to the west of that line, while Portugal had the same rights to all lands to the east of that line. Historians do not agree as to where exactly the line was drawn. Some say that it was 550 kilometres (350 miles) to the west of the Cape Verde Islands; others believe that it was drawn 1650 kilometres (1050 miles) to the west of these islands. Whichever it was, the fact is that the Portuguese were now free to explore along the routes which had been suggested by the work of the earlier explorers (pages 32-36).

AFRICAN TRADE

We have seen that the Portuguese built Fort Elmina in 1482 (picture 26). This was one step towards the creation of a Portuguese empire in Africa. Many people believe that until the white man went to Africa there was little, if any, industrial, commercial or social development in that vast continent. In fact, Africa was the centre for a number of thriving and prosperous kingdoms and empires. The Catalan Map (picture 28) shows that there was, in the fourteenth century, a prosperous trade in gold, ivory, silk and other produce. Dr Nkrumah, President of Ghana (1960-66), declared:

> Long before the slave trade and the imperialistic rivalries in Africa began, the civilizations of the Ghana Empire were in existence. At that time, in the ancient city of Timbuktu, Africans versed in science, arts and learning were having their works translated into Greek and Hebrew and were at the same time exchanging teachers with the University of Cordova, in Spain.

But the Portuguese were not content with the increased wealth which they gained from trade with African kingdoms. Their eyes were set on the route to the much more valuable spice trade.

DA GAMA

In 1497 the Portuguese king asked Diaz to draw up plans for an expedition which, it was hoped,

would reach India and, perhaps, the Spice Islands. When the four ships were finally prepared, command of the small fleet was given not to the experienced Diaz, but to the 28 year-old Vasco da Gama (picture 29). One of his crew kept a diary, in which he wrote:

In the year 1497, King Dom Manuel of Portugal, dispatched four vessels to make discoveries and go in search of spices. Vasco da Gama was the captain-major of these vessels; the S. Gabriel, the S. Rafael, the Berrio and the Goncalo Nunes.... We arrived at the island of Santiago in the Cape Verde Islands and anchored in the Bay of Santa Maria, where we took on board meat, water and wood and did the much needed repairs to our yards. On Thursday, 3rd August, we left in an easterly direction.

On Wednesday, 1st November, the day of All Saints, we perceived many indications of the neighbourhood of land including gulf weed which grows along the coast.

On Saturday, the 4th of the same month, a couple of hours before break of day, we made soundings in 110 fathoms [picture 30] ... and at nine o'clock we sighted the island of St. Helena.

At daybreak on Thursday, 16th November, having careened our ships and taken in wood, we set sail. At that time we did not know how far we might be below the Cape of Good Hope. We therefore stood out towards the south-south-west, and late on Saturday we beheld the Cape.

Along the way, the ships passed the prosperous Gold Coast and the Gulf of Benin, the centre of an already prospering trade. While, as the diarist noted, they carried out special tasks when they managed to land for a few days, the crew had many other tasks to tackle each day (picture 31). The dangers — from food poisoning, shipwreck and gales — were recalled by the diarist when he wrote about the rounding of the Cape:

On Sunday morning, 19th November, we once more made for the Cape, but were unable to round it for the wind was from the south-south-west, whilst the Cape juts out

30   Swinging the lead to determine the depth of water below the ship.

39

31 The captain supervising the crew as they go about their daily tasks.

towards the south-west. At last, on Wednesday at noon, having the wind astern, we succeeded in doubling the Cape and then ran along the coast. Late on Saturday, 25th November, the day of St. Catherine, we entered the bay of Sao Bras where we remained for thirteen days.

————————— SOUTH-EAST AFRICA —————————

So, once again, a Portuguese crew landed in Mossel Bay where Diaz had landed in 1486 (picture 25). Now came the unknown. Da Gama set off and kept close to the coast of East Africa (picture 32). As the diarist recorded, it was not all plain sailing:

. . . we sailed along the coast before a stern-wind, and when the wind swung round to the east we stood out to sea. And thus we kept making tacks until sunset on Tuesday, when the wind again veered to the west. We then lay to during the night . . . . In the morning we made straight for the land and at ten o'clock found ourselves once more at Cross Island that is 60 leagues [330 kilometres (208 miles)] behind our dead reckoning. This was due to the currents . . . which are very strong here.

That very day we again went forward by the route we had already attempted, and being favoured during three or four days by a strong sternwind, we were able to overcome the currents which we had feared might frustrate our plans . . . . By Christmas Day, we had discovered seventy leagues of coast . . .

If you read page 31 again you will see there that the ability to tack was one which the Portuguese ships enjoyed because of the variety and number of their sails. You might try and find on a map of modern Africa the name of the territory which the Portuguese discovered on Christmas Day 1497.

TO MOZAMBIQUE

The ships continued to make their way along the coast of East Africa (picture 32). The diarist provides us with a valuable picture of the people and the country and reminds us that the Africans were very prosperous:

> The captain thought that we should enter the bay [in Mozambique]. The people of this country are of ruddy complexion and well made. They are Mohammedans and their language is the same as that of the Moors. Their dresses are of fine linen or cotton stuffs, with variously coloured stripes, and of rich and elaborate workmanship. They wear toucas [caps] with borders of silk embroidered in gold. They are merchants, and trade with white Moors, four of whose vessels were at the time in port, laden with gold, silver, cloves, pepper, ginger and silver rings, as also with quantities of pearls, jewels and rubies, all of which articles are used by the people of this country.
>
> We were told, moreover, that Prester John resided not far from this place, and that the inhabitants of these cities were great merchants and owned big ships. The residence of Prester John was said to be far in the interior, and could only be reached on camels.

32   Vasco da Gama's voyage to India in 1497.

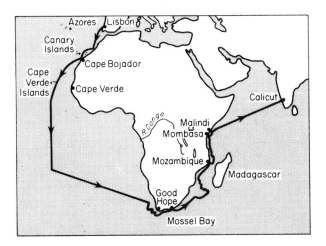

MOMBASA

In Mombasa (picture 34), the Portuguese faced a hostile reception from the Moors, who feared that the newcomers might take away their control of the African trade (picture 35). They might also have feared that the Christian Portuguese might have meant to try to convert them, by force perhaps, to Christianity:

> On Saturday, 7th April, we cast anchor off Mombasa but did not enter the port. No sooner had we been sighted than a dhow manned by Moors came out to us; in front of the city there lay numerous vessels all decked out in flags. And we, anxious not to be outdone, also dressed our ships. At midnight there approached us a dhow with about a hundred men, all armed with cutlasses and bucklers [shields]. When they reached the captain-major's vessel they attempted to board her, but only four or five of the most distinguished men among them were allowed to board.
>
> At night the captain-major questioned two Moors whom we had on board, by dropping boiling oil upon their skin, so that they might confess any treachery intended against us. They admitted that orders had been given to capture us as soon as we entered the port.
>
> About midnight two ships, with many men in them, approached. The ships stood off whilst the men entered the water, some swimming in the direction of the Berrio, others in that of the Rafael. Those who swam to the Berrio began to cut her cable. The men on watch thought at first that they were tunny fish but when they realised their mistake they shouted to the other vessels. The other swimmers had already got hold of the rigging of the mizzen-mast. Seeing themselves discovered they silently slipped down and fled. After the malice and treachery planned by these dogs had been discovered, we still remained on Wednesday and Thursday . . .

MALINDI

By the time da Gama had reached Malindi (picture 32), he had discovered that the Arabs, Africans and other traders were used to sailing across the Indian Ocean to the Indian mainland (picture 35). He wanted to get the service of one or more of the pilots who were used to sailing across what, to him, was the unknown ocean. However, the Muslim traders were unwilling to provide him with such a guide. So da Gama had to use force, as the diarist noted:

On the following Sunday, 22nd April, the king of Malindi's dhow brought on board one of his confidential servants; . . . the captain-major had this man seized and sent word to the king that he required the pilots whom he had promised. The king, when he received this message, sent a pilot [a Hindu from India called Ahmed ibn Majid] and the captain-major allowed the gentleman, whom he had retained in his vessel, to go away. We left Malindi on Tuesday, the 24th of the month, for a city called Calicut. . . . On the following Sunday, we once more saw the north star, which we had not seen for a long time.

INDIA AT LAST

In the next extract from the diary, you will see that da Gama and his men sailed in the Indian Ocean for 23 days. You might try to understand their fears of the unknown and the dangers they faced — of being becalmed perhaps, the problem of water supply in a very hot climate, and so on. The navigator with his astro-

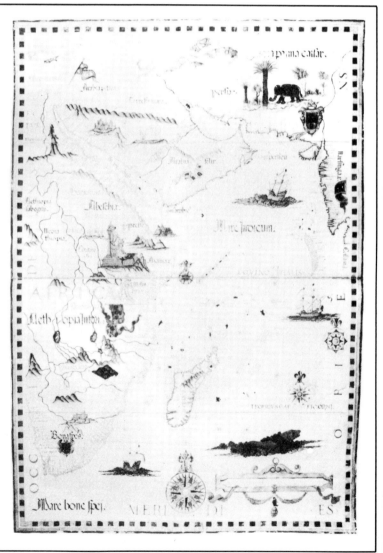

33 Diego Homen's map of 1558 (right) and extracts from it (left), showing an elephant and Prester John on his fabled throne.

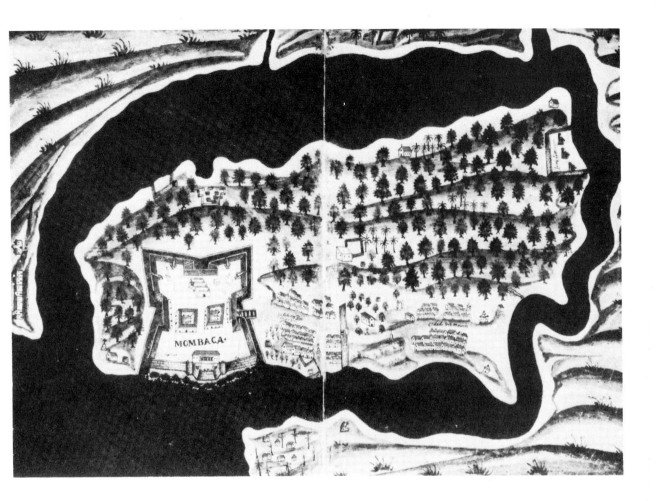

34 A map of Mombasa from an early sixteenth-century Portuguese book.

35 A map showing the trading links between Africa, India and the Far East.

labe (picture 36) must have been relieved when at last land was sighted:

On Friday, 18th May, after having seen no land for 23 days we sighted lofty mountains, and having all this time sailed before the wind we could not have made less than 600 leagues [3300 kilometres (2070 miles)]. That night we anchored two leagues [11 kilometres (7 miles)] from the city of Calicut which is inhabited by men of tawny complexion. Some of them have big beards and long hair, whilst others clip their hair short or shave the head, merely allowing a tuft to remain on the crown as a sign that they are Hindus. They also wear moustaches. They pierce their ears and wear much gold in them. They go naked down to the waist,

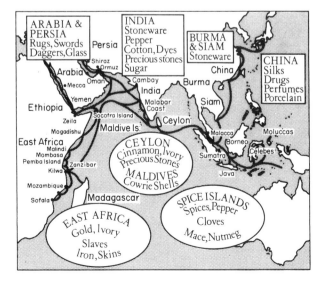

covering their lower extremities with fine cotton stuffs. But it is only the most respectable who do this, for the others manage as best they are able.

When we arrived, the king was fifteen leagues away. The captain-major sent two men to him with a message, informing him that an ambassador had arrived from the king of Portugal with letters, and that if he desired it, he would take them where the king then was.

The king presented the bearers of this message with much fine cloth. On the following morning, which was Monday, 28th May, the captain-major set out to speak to the king. . . . The captain, on entering, saluted in the manner of the country: by putting his hands together, then raising them towards Heaven . . . he [the king] invited him to address himself to the courtiers present. The captain-major replied that he was the ambassador of the king of Portugal and the bearer of a message which he could only deliver to him personally. In reply to this the king said that he was welcome, that for his part, he regarded him as a friend and brother, and would send ambassadors with him to Portugal.

On Wednesday morning the Moors returned, and took the captain to the palace. The palace was crowded with armed men. Our captain was kept waiting with his conductors for fully four long hours outside a door. When he entered, the king said that he had expected him on Tuesday. The captain said that the long road had tired him, and that for this reason he had not come to see him. The king replied that he had told him that he came from a very rich kingdom, and yet had brought him nothing. The king then asked him what he had come to discover: precious stones or men?

_____ TRADE _____

Da Gama was kept as hostage for a few days. The king agreed to release him on condition that the Portuguese sold some of their goods in exchange for spices. He also gave da Gama a letter for the King of Portugal: 'Vasca da Gama, a gentleman of your household, came to my country, whereat I was pleased. My country is rich in cinnamon, cloves, ginger, pepper and precious stones. That which I ask of you in exchange is gold, silver, corals and scarlet cloth.'

It seemed that the Portuguese had, indeed, found the source of that great spice trade which, it was hoped, would make the country — and its merchants — rich. However, there was the problem of overcoming the hostility of the Indian ruler. Da Gama realized that there was little he could do with only a small number of sailors. So, as the diarist noted, on 29 August 1498 they set out on the journey back:

On Wednesday, 29th [of August], the captain-major and the other captains agreed that, as we had discovered the country we had come in search of, as well as spices and precious stones, and since it appeared impossible to establish cordial relations with the people, it would be as well to make our departure. And it was resolved that we should take with us the Indians whom we had detained, as, on our return to Calicut, they might be useful to us in establishing friendly relations. We therefore set sail and left for Portugal, greatly rejoicing.

Owing to frequent calms and foul winds it took us three months less three days to cross this gulf, the Indian Ocean, and all our people again suffered from their gums, which grew over their teeth, so that they could not eat. Their legs and other parts of the body also swelled and these swellings spread until the sufferer died, without exhibiting symptoms of any other disease. Thirty of our men died in this manner — an equal number having died previously — and those able to navigate each ship were only seven or eight, and even these were not as well as they ought to have been. We had come to such a pass that all bonds of discipline had gone. Whilst suffering this affliction we addressed vows and petitions to the saints on behalf of our ships. The captains held council, and they agreed that if a favourable wind enabled us we would return to India whence we had come. But it pleased God in his mercy to send us a wind which in the course of six days carried us within sight of land.

In this extract the diarist reminds us of the great problems facing the men who sailed these vast distances in small ships in the days before anything was known of vitamins or the causes of scurvy.

36 An astrolabe which enabled the navigator to work out his position.

In September 1499, over a year after leaving India, da Gama arrived back at Lisbon. He had lost two of his ships and half the men on the remaining two ships had died. However, the valuable cargo brought a great profit to the King who had financed the expedition and acted as a spur to others to undertake similar expeditions. The diarist noted:

And the king, overjoyed at his coming, sent a nobleman and several gentlemen to bring him to court; where, being arrived through crowds of spectators, he was received with extraordinary honour. For this glorious service, the privilege of being called Don was given to his family; to his Coat of Arms was added part of the king's. He had a pension of three thousand ducats yearly, and he was afterwards presented to greater honours for his services in the Indies.

THE YOUNG HISTORIAN

1   On your map of the world mark the route taken by da Gama.
2   Write the headlines which might have appeared above reports on:
    (a) The division of the world by the Pope, in a Portuguese newspaper;
    (b) The departure, without Diaz, in a Portuguese newspaper;
    (c) The arrival in Mozambique, in an Arab newspaper;
    (d) The arrival in Calicut, in an Indian newspaper;
    (e) The arrival back in Lisbon, in a Portuguese newspaper.
3   What evidence is there in the text and in the illustrations that the Africans were very prosperous in the fifteenth century? (Pictures 28, 32, 33, 34 and 35 will be useful.)
4   Write the account which a newspaper reporter might have written if he had been with da Gama and his men at Santa Maria (page 39).
5   Imagine that you are one of da Gama's men, recounting in old age the story of the voyage. What pleasures and what dangers would you most recall?
6   Draw or paint: (a) swinging the lead (picture 30); (b) the arrival at Mombasa; (c) the caravels set out.
7   Write short playlets based on: (a) preparing for the expedition; (b) da Gama at Calicut; (c) da Gama and his men quarrel on the journey home.

FURTHER HELP

Books
Addison, John, *Ancient Africa* (Rupert Hart-Davis)
And the books recommended in the previous chapter, page 36.

Filmstrip
See the previous chapter, page 36.

COLUMBUS AND THE ROUTE VIA THE WEST TO THE EAST

COLUMBUS'S EARLY CAREER

Christopher Columbus (picture 37) was born in the Italian port of Genoa, which was the main rival to Marco Polo's home port of Venice (pages 21-22). His father was a prosperous weaver and, according to Christopher's son, Ferdinand, was able to pay for Christopher to go to the famous

37   Christopher Columbus.

University of Padua, where he studied geometry, astronomy and map-making. However, Columbus himself wrote about having gone to sea when he was only fourteen — so perhaps he did not go to University at all. What we do know for sure is that by the time he was twenty he was sailing in Genoese trading ships, to and from the ports of the eastern Mediterranean (picture 13) in ships resembling those in which the Venetians sailed (picture 12).

Trade rivalry between Venice and Genoa often led to fighting between these two city-states. When Columbus was twenty-five, he was on board a Genoese ship which was sunk off Cape St Vincent. He managed to reach the Portuguese mainland and make his way to Lisbon, where he settled. We know that he read Marco Polo's book and that he knew about the travels of Diaz (page 36). In his own writings, Columbus tells us about the study he made while in Lisbon — of maps and map-making, astronomy, and the details of the journeys so far made by the Portuguese (pages 32-36).

HIS AMBITIONS

Columbus had made two voyages to the west coast of Africa and had discovered for himself that the stories about African wealth and prosperity (pictures 28 and 33) were quite true. He realized that there was gold for the taking if only one knew where to look for it. But, like many other sailors and merchants, Columbus had his mind on the even greater wealth that was thought to exist in far-off Cathay, the name given to Marco Polo's China. Columbus had the idea that if he could be the one to find the route to that source of wealth he could become both famous and wealthy. He also believed that he might be able to convert the Chinese to Christianity. He wrote: 'In the New Heaven and Earth which our Lord made He made me, Christoval Colon, the messenger and showed me where to go'.

He studied the various maps then available (picture 18) and thought that he had worked out a new way to get to China and the valuable Spice Islands — by sailing westwards across the Atlantic, around the world and so to China. He thought he had worked out a method of calculating the distance covered by one degree of longitude (see page 53) while he was on a voyage to Africa. This, he thought, was 73 kilometres (45⅔ miles). Using this figure as a basis, he

48

reckoned that Japan lay just to the west of the Azores (picture 42), about 4500 kilometres (2800 miles) to the west of the Canaries (picture 42), so that China was only about 6700 kilometres (4200 miles) away. Unfortunately for him his first piece of arithmetic was wrong. Japan was 16 600 kilometres (10 400 miles) and China 18 900 kilometres (11 800 miles) away from the Canaries.

AID FROM SPAIN

Columbus took his plans to the King of Portugal, who dismissed them as impractical and much less sure of success than were the plans for finding a route via the Cape (pages 32-36 and 37-45). He then turned to the rulers of Spain, Ferdinand and Isabella. They agreed to see him in 1489, but although they were prepared to listen to him, they were more concerned with ridding Spain of the Moors than with financing risky ventures overseas. In 1492, the Moors were finally defeated (picture 38) and there was time to bring Columbus back to the royal court. Isabella liked, in particular, the idea of helping to convert the Chinese to Christianity and, as one historian wrote: 'I will assume the undertaking,' said she, 'for my own crown of Castile, and am ready to pawn my jewels to defray the expenses of it, if the funds of the treasury shall be found inadequate.'

PREPARING THE EXPEDITION

Columbus asked Isabella to make him Admiral of the Ocean Seas, Viceroy and Governor-General of all the territories claimed in the name of Spain. He also wanted one-tenth of the profits he hoped to make from the expedition and to be allowed to be an investor in future (and, hopefully, profitable) expeditions. By 17 April 1492, the Queen had accepted these extravagant claims and gave Columbus a letter which he was to present to the Grand Khan (picture 11). By the middle of May, he was in Palos, near Cadiz, which was to provide him with two ships in payment of a debt which the townspeople owed the Queen. It took ten weeks to find the third ship, get together the crews, stores and equipment.

As an inducement to men to volunteer for the dangerous journey into the unknown, the Queen issued an order that if anyone who

38 This is part of a carved altar piece in the Royal Chapel in Granada, Spain, whose walls and turrets can be seen in the background. Moorish prisoners file out from the gates (right of picture) of the Alhambra, while their leader Boabdil (extreme left) makes his way to hand over the keys of the city to the Christians who, under Ferdinand and Isabella, have finally defeated the Moors.

was waiting to be tried for some crime sailed with Columbus, a royal pardon would be granted to that person. So among the hundred or so who sailed in the three small caravels (picture 22) were a large number of criminals — not the type that would be best suited to the dangers facing them. Then, as Columbus wrote:

> I left the city of Granada on the 12th day of May, in the year 1492, and came to the town of Palos, which is a seaport, where I equipped three vessels well suited for such service [the *Santa Maria* of 100 tons, the *Nina* of 60 tons, and the *Pinta* of about 40 tons], and departed from that port well supplied with provisions and with many sailors on the 3rd day of August of the same year, being Friday, half an hour before sunrise, taking the route to the Canary Islands . . .

There were 18 men on board the *Pinta* and another 18 on the *Nina*. His own ship, the *Santa Maria* (picture 40), carried about 60 men.

_____ PROBLEMS _____

Within three months Columbus had run into trouble. As his chronicler noted:

Monday, 6th August   The rudder of the caravel *Pinta* became unhinged and Martin Alonzo Pinzon, who was in command, believed or suspected that it was a contrivance of Gomez Rascon and Cristobal Quintero, to whom the caravel belonged, for they dreaded to go on this voyage. The Admiral says that before they sailed these men had been grumbling and making difficulties. The Admiral was much disturbed at not being able to help the *Pinta* without danger, and he says that he was eased to some anxiety when he reflected that Martin Alonzo Pinzon was a man of energy and ingenuity.

Columbus's sense of vision and adventure was not shared by all who sailed with him. They put into the Canaries (picture 42) to repair the *Pinta* and then hardly had they set sail again before Columbus was told that the Portuguese were trying to stop the voyage. The chronicler wrote:

Between 10th-31st August they repaired the *Pinta* thoroughly .... They fitted the *Pinta* with square sails for she was lateen rigged. It is said that the *Nina* was rerigged at the same time.

Thursday, 6th September   Having taken on water, wood and meat, he finally made sail from the island of Gomara. The Admiral learned that there were three Portuguese caravels cruising about looking for him — this must have been because the King of Portugal was angry that the Admiral should have served the King and Queen of Spain.

There is no evidence that Columbus ran into the Portuguese. Indeed, he had enough trouble as it was, without having to fight off an armed enemy. If you read pages 42-45 again you will

40   In the centre is the *Santa Maria*, which was about 20 metres (60 feet) in length. The *Pinta*, on the right, was about half that size, weighing only 50 tons. The *Nina*, on the left, was still smaller and had a crew of only 23.

41 Columbus takes his leave of the two monarchs.

understand some of the problems facing men
who sailed on these long voyages. Mouldy food,
stale water, damp clothes, cramped living
conditions — all combined to make life on
board unhealthy, uncomfortable and sometimes
fatal (page 45). The men who sailed with
Columbus faced a hazard which the Portuguese
sailors had not known. How long were they
going to be away from land? According to
Columbus's arithmetic, there were about 4800
kilometres (3000 miles) or so to go after leaving
the Canaries. But as they sailed along, through

42 Columbus's route.

52

September, some men began to think that they would never reach land again. Others began to work out the arithmetic for themselves, noting how many days they had been travelling and how far they travelled each day. Columbus tried to put these men off the scent by reporting a false figure for each day's journey:

Sunday 9th September   This day the Admiral calculated that we had run 19 leagues but he decided to record less than this number so that the crew would not be terrified and disheartened if the voyage was of long duration.

Sunday 16th September   The Admiral says that on the day and ever afterwards, they met with temperate breezes so that there was great pleasure in enjoying the mornings, which only lacked the song of the nightingales. He says that the weather was like April in Andalusia.

On into the unknown they sailed (picture 42), through the Saragossa Sea where the sight of weed and the capture of live crabs brought fresh hopes that they had come within reach of land. From 20 September, however, they were becalmed, and they feared being marooned until they died from thirst or starvation. Fortunately, a wind sprang up: 'Saturday 22nd September   This head wind was very necessary for me because my people were much alarmed at the thought that in these seas no wind ever blew in the direction of Spain.'

Twice there were reports by men who claimed to have sighted land; each time the reports proved to be false. Men's hopes, having been raised, fell back even further. On 10 October a mutiny broke out:

Wednesday 10th October   Here the people could bear no more. They complained of the length of the voyage. But the Admiral cheered them up in the best way he could by giving them high hopes of the advantages they might gain. He added that, however much they might complain, he had to go to the Indies, and that he would go on until he found them with the help of our Lord.

Columbus wrote: 'I calculate landfall at Cathay at any hour. But the men fear we have sailed too far South and missed Asia altogether.' He promised the men that if they hadn't sighted land within two or three days he would turn back. But in his own log he wrote: 'I will continue until I find them.'

Fortunately for Columbus and for the mutinous and fearful men, things changed for the better on the very next day:

Thursday 11th October   The crew of the caravel *Nina* saw signs of land, and a small branch covered with berries. Everyone breathed afresh and rejoiced at these signs. The land was first seen by a sailor named Rodrigo de Triana [picture 43].

On the following morning Columbus and his men landed (picture 44).

Friday 12th October   The vessels were hove to, waiting for daylight. They arrived at a small island called in the language of the Indians, Guanahani [San Salvador or, today, Watling Island]. Presently they saw naked people. The Admiral went on shore in the armed boat, with Martin Pinzon, and Vincente Yanez, the captain of the *Nina*. The Admiral took the royal standard.

On the beach, with the natives watching, Columbus knelt and prayed: 'O Lord, Almighty and Everlasting God, Thou hast created the Heaven and the Earth and the Sea, blessed and glorified be Thy Name and praised be Thy Majesty which hath helped Thy Humble servants, that Thy Holy Name may be proclaimed in this second part of the Earth.'

The chronicler recalls his impressions of their newly discovered land: 'Having landed, they saw very green trees, and many streams of water, and fruits of many kinds. The Admiral called to the others that they should bear faithful witness that he, in the presence of all, had taken possession of the island for the King and for the Queen.'

Here are the actual words of the Admiral:

They appeared to me to be a race of very poor people. They go as naked as when their mothers bore them, even the women. All whom I saw were youths, none more than 30 years of age. They are very well made with handsome bodies, and very good faces. Their hair is short and coarse, almost like the hair of a horse's tail. They paint themselves black but are the colour of the Canary Islanders neither black nor white. They neither carry nor know anything of weapons, for I showed them swords, and they cut themselves through

43 An artist's idea of the discovery of America.

ignorance. They would make good, intelligent servants, for I observed that they quickly took in what was said to them, and I believe that they could easily become Christians as they appear to have no religion [picture 44].

Columbus named the place at which they landed San Salvador, and claimed it in the name of Spain. He believed that he had landed in one of the islands that, he reckoned, lay to the east of Japan. Their poverty, he thought, was

54

due to the frequent raids made on them by the Khan's warriors. He found enough gold to make him think that it was worthwhile making more journeys round the neighbouring islands in the hope that he would come to the Chinese mainland. He wrote:

44 Columbus setting foot in the New World and being greeted by natives whom he called Indians.

I here propose to leave to circumnavigate this island until I may have speech with this King and see if I can obtain from him the gold that I heard he has, and afterwards to depart for another much larger island which I believe must be Japan according to the description of these Indians whom I carry, and which they call Colba, in which they say that there are ships and sailors both

many and great; and beyond this is another island which they call Bofio, which also they say is very big; and the others which are between we shall see as we pass, and according as I shall find a collection of gold or spicery, I shall decide what I have to do. But in any case I am determined to go to the mainland and to the city of Quinsay [picture 17] and to present your Highness's letters to the Grand Khan, and to beg a reply and come home with it.

The island of Colba to which Columbus refers was, in fact, Cuba, where he recorded the following: 'And from that point; I sent two men inland to learn if there were a king or great cities. They travelled for three days and found an infinite number of small hamlets and people without number, but nothing of importance.'

Cuba was a beautiful island, but, unfortunately for Columbus, the Spaniards discovered no gold. Columbus continued to believe that China was bound to be nearby:

Without doubt, there is in these islands a vast quantity of gold, and the Indians I have on board do not speak without reason when they say that in these islands are places where they dig up gold, and wear it on their necks, ears, arms, legs; the rings are very large. There are also precious stones, pearls, and an infinity of spices .... There is also a great quantity of cotton and I believe it would sell well here in the cities of the Great Khan (which will be discovered without doubt) without sending it to Spain.

TROUBLE

Some Spanish criminal-sailors, led by Pinzon on whom Columbus had earlier relied (page 51), sailed away in the *Pinta* on 21 November. As Columbus wrote in a letter to Ferdinand and Isabella: 'Martin Pinzon of the *Pinta* deserted this night. I believe he has gone to seek gold in an island to the south. He has always been a rebellious and avaricious man. I trust your Highnesses will not forget his treason.'

Some of the remaining sailors tried to make money for themselves by cheating the native people. The chronicler noted:

. . . the Admiral sent six men to a large village because the Chief had come the day before and said that he had some pieces of gold. When the Christians arrived, the Secretary of the Admiral took the Chief by the hand. The Admiral had sent him to prevent the others from cheating the Indians. As the Indians are so simple, and the Spanish so avaricious and grasping, they are not satisfied that the Indians should give them all they want in exchange for a bead or a bit of glass, but the Spanish would take everything without any return at all. The Admiral always forbids this, although with the exception of gold, the things given by the Indians are of little value.

SHIPWRECKED

Now the commander of only two ships, Columbus sailed away from Cuba intending to make a map of the various islands in the region. On 24 December he handed over the watch at eleven o'clock at night. Then:

Tuesday 25th December As it was calm, the sailor who steered the ship [the *Santa Maria*] thought he would go to sleep, leaving the tiller in charge of a boy. It pleased our Lord that at 12 o'clock at night, when the Admiral had retired to rest, and all had fallen asleep, seeing that it was a dead calm and the sea like glass, the current carried the ship onto one of the sandbanks [actually a coral reef]. The Admiral at once rushed up on deck and presently, the master of the ship, whose watch it was, came up. The Admiral ordered him and others to launch the boat to run an anchor out astern but they tried to take refuge in the caravel [the *Nina*]. The caravel's crew would not let them on board, and they therefore returned to the ship. When the Admiral saw that his own people fled in this way, he ordered the masts to be cut down and the ship to be lightened as much as possible to see if she would come off. But as the water continued to rise, nothing more could be done. Then the timbers opened and the ship was lost.

Columbus used this shipwreck as the excuse for founding a permanent base. He wrote:

I have taken possession of a large town on the island of Hispaniola to which I have given the name Villa de Navidad [Christmas Town] and in it I have built a fort. Its situation is most convenient as it is well placed for the gold mines and for taking part in the trading of this island as well as that of the mainland belonging to the Great Khan.

His chronicler noted:

Friday, 4th January 1493　He left on that island of Hispaniola 39 men in the fortress and says that they were great friends of the Guacanageri [the Indians] .... He left behind all the merchandise which had been provided for bartering, which was a lot so that they could trade for gold. He also left a year's supply of bread, wines and much artillery as well as the ship's boat so that they, most of them being sailors, might go, when it was convenient, to search for the gold mine. They were also able to find a good site for a town, for this was not a desirable port. He also left seeds, for sowing, and his officers, the Alquazil and Secretary, as well as ship's carpenter, a caulker, a good gunner well acquainted with artillery, a cooper, a physician and a tailor, all being seamen as well.

THE JOURNEY BACK HOME

On 6 January Pinzon in the *Pinta* returned, claiming that he had been forced by a mutinous crew to desert Columbus in November. Columbus's chronicler noted: 'He decided to return home as quickly as possible to get rid of such an evil company with whom he thought it necessary to dissemble, although they were a mutinous set ... for it was not a fitting time to deal out punishment.'

Columbus put a few Indians and some gold on the *Nina* and *Pinta* and on 14 January the two ships set out for home:

Monday 14th February　This night the wind increased and the waves were terrible, rising against each other, and so shaking and straining the vessel that she could make no headway and was in danger of being stove in. Seeing the great danger, the Admiral began to run before it .... The Admiral ordered that a pilgrimage should be made to Our Lady of Guadeloupe ... and that all the crew should take an oath that the pilgrimage should be made by the man on whom the lot fell. As many beans as there were persons on board were obtained and on one a cross was cut with a knife. They were then put into

a cap and shaken up. The first who put in his hand was the Admiral, and he drew out the bean with a cross so that the lot fell on him.

The two ships were separated by this storm which so frightened the crew of Columbus's *Nina* that they all swore to make a pilgrimage if they should come through safely. When they reached the Azores (picture 42) Columbus sent half the crew to carry out their vow:

Sunday 17th February　Half of the crew then went in their shirts to carry out their vow. While they were at their prayers, all the people of the town, the cavalry and the foot soldiers with a captain at their head, came and took them all prisoner. The Admiral, suspecting nothing, was waiting for the boat to take him and the rest to fulfil their vow. At 11 o'clock, seeing that they did not come back he weighed anchor, and made sail until he was in full view of the chapel. He saw many of the horsemen dismount and get into the boat with their weapons. They came out to the caravel to seize the Admiral so that there was no other remedy but to go to sea. As there was a strong wind and a high sea, the Admiral says he was in much anxiety because he had only three sailors who knew their business. Soon afterwards the boat came alongside with five sailors, two priests and a scrivener who asked to be shown the commission granted them by the sovereigns of Castile. Then the Portuguese went on shore contented, and presently released all the crew and the boat.'

The enmity of the Portuguese, to whom the Azores belonged, was not the last trouble to confront the unlucky Columbus. Having set sail again:

Sunday 24th February　A squall hit the *Nina*, split all her sails and put the rest of the vessel in great danger. Afterwards they ran under bare poles, owing to the force of the gale and the heavy sea.

HOME AGAIN

However, the small ship with a tired crew finally reached Portugal (picture 45):

Monday 4th March　During the night they were exposed to a terrible storm and expected

45   The triumphant Columbus before the two monarchs on his return from his first journey.

to be overwhelmed by the cross-seas. The wind seemed to raise the caravel high in the air, and there was rain and lightning in several directions. When it was light, the Admiral recognized the land, which was the rock of Cintra, near the river of Lisbon, and decided to run in because there was nothing else he could do. Presently, the Admiral wrote to the King of Portugal stating that the sovereigns of Castile had ordered him to enter the ports of his Highness, to ask for what he required.

On 15 March, Columbus anchored in the Rio Tinto at Palos, where he found Pinzon and the *Pinta* waiting for him. Pinzon died within a week of the return and so escaped the punishment which Columbus hoped to serve on him for his treachery. When he reached Barcelona, Columbus received a great welcome from people who still shared his great hopes. In a letter to Ferdinand and Isabella he wrote:

The humble gifts which I bring to your Highnesses will give you some idea of the wealth of these regions. Doubters may say I exaggerate the amount of gold and spices to be found, and, in truth, we have only yet seen a hundredth of the splendour of these kingdoms . . . . I know that huge mines of gold will be found if your Highnesses allow me to return . . .

THE YOUNG HISTORIAN

1 On your map of the world mark the route taken by Columbus.
2 Write the headlines which might have appeared above reports on:
(a) The rivalry between Genoa and Venice (in papers of each city-state);
(b) Columbus's idea of the distance to China — in a Portuguese newspaper;
(c) The departure of Columbus's expedition;
(d) The news of the discovery — in a native paper and in a Spanish paper;
(e) The arrival home of the successful Columbus.
3 Explain why Ferdinand and Isabella were prepared to support Columbus.
4 Write short playlets on:
(a) Columbus's appeal to Ferdinand and Isabella (picture 39);
(b) Preparing the expedition (page 48 and pictures 40-42);
(c) The plan of a mutiny against Columbus and how he dealt with it (page 53);
(d) Sighting land and the first landing (pictures 43 and 44);
(e) The journey home (page 57).
5 Make your own illustrations with titles:
(a) A shipwreck (picture 27); (b) Columbus in the New World (picture 44).

6 Write the letters which might have been written by:
(a) Columbus, explaining why he wanted to get to China;
(b) One of his crew: (i) before they set out, (ii) after they had arrived in the New World, and (iii) on their arrival back in Spain.

FURTHER HELP

Books
Hobley, L.F., *Exploring the Americas* (Methuen)
Kaufman, M., *Christopher Columbus* (Muller)
McKendrick, M., *Ferdinand and Isabella* (Cassell Caravel)
Wilcox, D., *Explorers* (BBC Publications)
Wymer, N., *Great Explorers* (Oxford University Press)

Film
Christopher Columbus (Gateway)

Filmstrip
Christopher Columbus (available from Gateway, Hulton, Wills and Hepworth, and Visual Publications)

ROUND THE WORLD WITH MAGELLAN'S MEN

Ferdinand Magellan (picture 46) was born in 1480, the son of a wealthy nobleman. In 1493, he became a page at the court of King John II who had supported Diaz's work (pages 33-35).

While Magellan was at the royal court, Columbus had undertaken the first of his voyages (pages 48-58) and da Gama had found the eastern route by sea to India (pages 37-46). In 1505, Magellan was a member of a huge expedition sent out by Portugal, under the leadership of Francis d'Almeida. There were 20 or more huge galleons as well as many smaller vessels which would be used — it was hoped — to patrol the Indian coast. About 2000 sailors and soldiers were specially trained for this voyage, which was intended to result in the conquest of parts of India and the setting up of a large Portuguese empire.

The aim was to put an end to European dependence on the old trade routes through the eastern Mediterranean, where Turkish pirates (picture 47) made the difficult work even more hazardous. However, the Portuguese found that while some African chiefs welcomed them, more were hostile. They also suffered the loss of many of their ships in the storms which swept along the west coast of Africa (picture 27). Nevertheless, they reached the Cape by the end of June 1505, made their way up the east coast of Africa, building forts to protect Portuguese traders (picture 26), and left some ships patrolling this coast. By the end of February 1506, they had conquered a stretch of the Indian coast and set up their capital in Cochin. In a series of naval battles, the Portuguese defeated fleets sent out by Arab kings and traders, and by 1509 Portugal was in command of the Indian Ocean.

Magellan was selected as one of the crew of 70 of a galleon which took part in an attack on Malacca in 1509 (picture 53). This expedition was a failure, largely owing to the carelessness of the commander and the treachery of the Sultan of Malacca. Magellan, however, became better known as the result of his bravery during a skirmish with the troops of the Sultan of Malacca and because of his work in preventing a mutiny among the sailors during the voyage back to Portugal. In 1511 Magellan, now a junior officer, was a member of another expedition to capture the Straits of Malacca (picture 53). This time the Portuguese succeeded; Malacca was captured and the route to the Spice Islands (pictures 48 and 53) was now open. Magellan returned to Portugal and in 1513 served in the Portuguese army, which was sent to put down a rebellion among the Moroccan Moors. In this, his career was somewhat like that of Prince Henry (picture 20). Magellan was wounded during a battle and had a permanent limp as a result. More seriously, he was accused of having stolen some of the booty taken after the capture of the Moorish stronghold. The King never found out what had happened to the booty, but he turned against Magellan, who left the royal court.

A friend of Magellan's, Francis Serrana, had remained behind in the Spice Islands and letters from him drew Magellan to the idea of leading a trading expedition to those islands. For two years after leaving the royal court, Magellan studied maps, sailors' reports, astronomy and navigation in Lisbon.

Although Columbus had failed to get to the mainland of America (pages 47-58), his success had inspired others to venture out. Amerigo

FERDINANDVS MAGELLANVS FRETI PERVVIANI TERRÆQVE AVSTRALIS INVENTOR ✝

MONVMENTA LO: QVENTVR.

46 Magellan.

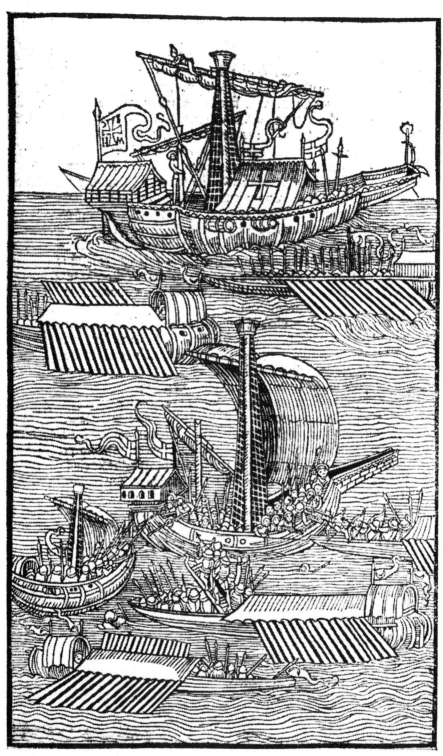

Vespucci had reached the coast of Brazil in 1499, and in 1501 he had travelled along the coast of South America from Cape San Roque to Patagonia, a distance of over 4800 kilometres (3000 miles). Vespucci was the first to prove that America was not a part of Asia, as Columbus had thought, but was a land mass of its own. Magellan read some of Vespucci's work about his journeys and about the new lands which had become known as America, after Vespucci's first name. Ruiz Faleiro, an astronomer friend of his, persuaded Magellan that although America stretched far to the south there would be a route round its southernmost tip to the Spice Islands (picture 48).

THE EXPEDITION

In 1517, Magellan went to Spain where he married. His father-in-law introduced him to the King of Spain, Charles V, who was attracted by the idea of finding a route to the Spice Islands. He wanted to try to put an end to the Portuguese domination of affairs in the east. In March 1518, he agreed to provide Magellan with five ships and a crew of 234 men. He also agreed to give Magellan one-fifth of the profits that might be made by the expedition and to allow him and other officers special privileges in future trade with these islands.

48   A map drawn in 1500 showing that the map-maker had some idea that there was a continent beyond Hispaniola. Notice again the African section of this map which shows the Niger flowing across the African continent.

It took eighteen months to repair the five ships. Magellan wrote: 'They are very old and patched. I would be sorry to sail even as far as the Canaries in them [picture 42], for their ribs are as soft as butter.'

Magellan took as much as could be carried, aware of the problems facing men sailing in small caravels along a hazardous route. There were 9800 kilos of biscuit, 2 310 kilos of gunpowder, 258 kilos of salt beef, 238 dozen fried fish, 200 barrels of sardines, 508 kilos of cheese and 216 kilos of oil as well as beans, peas, lentils, flour, honey, onions, figs and salt. Finally, as his chronicler wrote:

. . . after all the preparations had been made, the Captain-General . . . kept the destination of the voyage a secret so that the crew would not be filled with fear. The masters and captains of the other ships hated the Captain-General greatly . . . because he was a Portuguese and they were Spaniards; these people have been rivals and borne each other ill will for a long time . . .

On Monday 10 August in 1519, the fleet carrying 237 men in five ships, the *San Antonio* [120 tons], the *Trinidad* [110 tons], the *Concepcion* [90 tons], the *Victoria* [85 tons, picture 49] and the *Santiago* [75 tons] was ready to set sail from Seville.

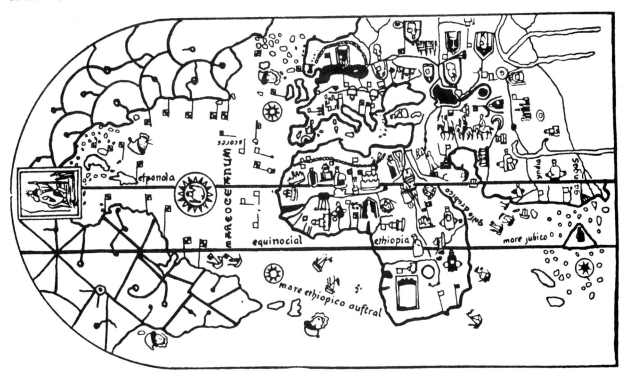

We came to the mouth of the river Guadalquivir carrying sail only on the foremast and firing all our artillery. At St. Lucar, the captain ordered all the men . . . to go to confession . . . he leading the way. We set sail from St. Lucar and on 26th September arrived at the Canary Islands [picture 50] where we remained three and a half days taking in provisions . . . . After that we sailed to a port called Monterose where we stayed for two days supplying ourselves with pitch.

Sometimes we had contrary winds, sometimes we had good winds and at other times

50 Magellan's route and the route from the Philippines along which the *Victoria* sailed without its famous captain.

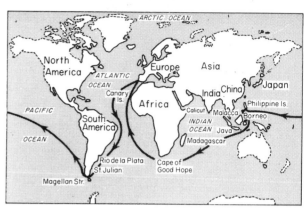

49 Magellan's ship *Victoria*, **which sailed round the world.**

VICTORIA

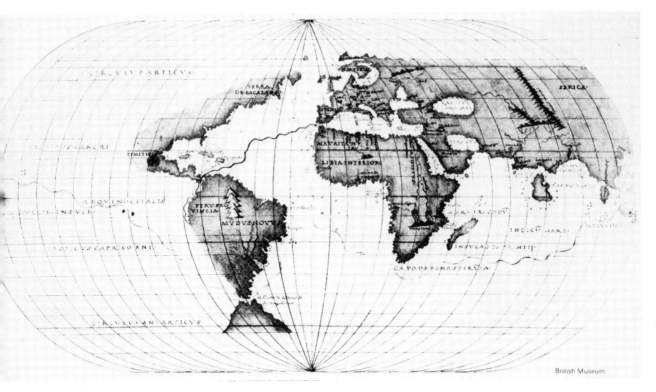

51 A map drawn after Magellan's death, bearing all the signs that his voyage had changed men's ideas of the shape of their world.

British Museum

we had rain and no wind. We sailed for 60 days before we reached the equator .... We crossed to a place called Verzin where we obtained fresh victuals ...

SOUTH AMERICA

The modern map showing the route taken by Magellan (picture 50) does not show that they spent almost a year making their way along the coast of South America. They spent a fortnight in Rio de Janeiro where they picked up supplies of fresh food. The chronicler noted:

> We made excellent bargains .... For a hook or a knife we purchased five or six fowls; a comb brought us two geese; and a small looking-glass or a pair of scissors, as much fish as would serve ten people .... Our playing cards were an equally advantageous object of barter; for a king of spades I obtained half-a-dozen fowls.

They probably consulted a map such as the one shown in picture 51, which was drawn in 1536 and which shows the route taken by Magellan. They left Rio on Boxing Day 1520 and made their way up to the River Plate. At first, they imagined that they had found the strait which would open the route to the Spice Islands. However, after days of sailing up the great river they realized their mistake and once again turned along the coast of South America until they reached Port St Julian in March 1520. Magellan decided to stay in this safe harbour until the worst of winter was over. They met some of the natives, described by the chronicler as 'naked giants' who 'capered almost naked on the sands'. The marks left in the sand by the feet of these jumping giants resembled the footmarks left by bears, and so Magellan christened these people Patagonians, after the Spanish word for 'bear'.

During their long stay in Port St Julian, the Portuguese had to fight off some unfriendly natives. More seriously, Magellan had to deal with treachery on the part of four of his captains who had been bribed by the Portuguese to put an end to the expedition. Magellan dealt with this plot by flaying one of the plotters until he died, by ordering the second to be stabbed, and by leaving the other two behind when he sailed from Patagonia.

65

During their stay at Port St Julian, Magellan had sent his ships to explore along the coast. One of them, the *Santiago*, was lost in a shipwreck (picture 27) although the men were all saved. So only four small ships continued the journey southwards. On 21 October 1520, they found the strait for which they were looking (picture 52). We have to read the words of Magellan's chronicler in order to get some idea of the very real dangers that were faced by these men in their small ships as they sailed into the unknown. They first had to explore this newly discovered opening:

. . . The whole of the crew were so firmly persuaded that this strait had no western outlet that we should not, but for the Captain-General, have ventured on its exploration. As soon as we entered on this water the Captain sent forward two vessels, the *San Antonio* and *Concepcion*, to examine where it terminated, or whither it led, while we in the *Trinidad* and the *Victoria* awaited them in the mouth.

At night came on a terrible hurricane, which lasted six and thirty hours, and forced us to quit our anchors and leave our vessels to the mercy of the winds and waves in the gulf. The two other vessels, equally buffeted, were unable to double a cape to rejoin us; the gale drove them toward what they conceived to be the bottom of a bay. They were apprehensive of being driven ashore, but at the instant they gave themselves up for lost they saw a small opening, which they took for an inlet of the bay. Into this they entered . . .

Two days passed without the vessels returning . . . . Then we saw them advancing towards us under full sail, and their flags flying; and when sufficiently near, heard the report of their bombards and their loud exclamations of joy. We repeated the salutation, and when we learnt from them that they had seen the strait we made toward them to continue our voyage.

Magellan not only had to face storms and the natural fear of facing the unknown. He also had to suffer from even more treachery. When the four ships were well into the strait they came across two openings, one to the south-east and the other to the south-west. Magellan sent the *San Antonio* and the *Concepcion* to explore the channel to the south-east, while the other two ships explored the route to the south-west. The captain-pilot of the *San Antonio*, who resented the fact that a Portuguese — Magellan — was in command of a Spanish expedition, and who also believed that the whole enterprise was doomed to fail, decided to return home to Spain. Magellan spent several days searching for the missing vessel. While this fruitless search was going on, a party of men was sent in a small boat to seek the end of the second channel. It was this small group who found the way into the new ocean — the Pacific Ocean — on the other side of South

52 The Straits of Magellan as drawn in a book published in 1600. Notice the compass on the left, which shows that the American mainland is near the bottom of this drawing.

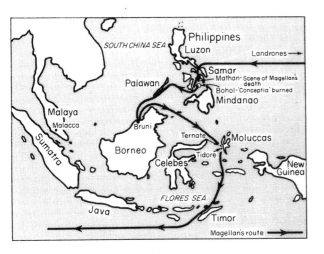

53 The Philippines, East Indies and Malaysia, showing some of the places mentioned in this chapter.

America. It has taken them 38 days to sail along the 650 kilometres (400 miles) of the rocky strait between the snow-capped mountains on the north and the barren Tierra del Fuego on the south.

THE PACIFIC OCEAN

On 28 November 1520, the three ships sailed into the peaceful waters, which they called Pacific (after the Portuguese word for 'peace'). But they had spent a good deal of time getting through the stormy straits and their food supplies were running low. They then had a journey of three months and 20 days without being able to get any new supplies. Conditions on board the small caravels were harsh at the best of times (page 45). Magellan's men suffered more than usual difficulties and had no idea how long their journey might last. The chronicler wrote:

> The biscuit we were eating was nothing but dust and worms . . . . The water . . . was putrid and offensive. We . . . ate pieces of the leather with which the mainyard was covered . . . . These pieces of leather were so hard that they required being soaked in the sea in order to render them supple; after this we broiled them to eat. Frequently, indeed, we were obliged to subsist on sawdust and even mice . . . . Our greatest misfortune was being attacked by a malady in which the gums swelled so as to hide the teeth . . . . Those affected thus were incapable of chewing their food.

Nineteen men died from the dreaded scurvy, and another 30 or so were so stricken by the disease as to be unfit for work. It is small wonder that the chronicler wrote: 'If Our Lord and his Mother had not aided us we should all have died of hunger in this vast sea; I think no man will ever perform such a voyage again.'

THE PHILIPPINES

At last the three ships reached the group of islands which we now call the Philippines. As you can see from picture 53, these are to the north of the Moluccas or Spice Islands which Magellan hoped to reach. The explorers were well received by the native people, whom they baptised into the Christian faith. They exchanged cloth, knives and mirrors for fresh food. They showed the native king of Massava island how a gun worked and allowed the native people to stab at them with their knives to show that a man dressed in armour was worth over a hundred natives. Magellan then led his ships to the island of Cebu, where they opened a shop and sold iron, cloth and other goods in exchange for gold, rice, pigs, goats and other provisions. At first, Magellan got on well with the King of Cebu. But on 27 April 1521 a chief of another island gathered an army of 1 500 to attack the newcomers:

> They showered on us such clouds of bamboo lances . . . that it was with difficulty that we defended ourselves. Some threw spears headed with iron at our Captain-General, who . . . ordered away a party of our men to set fire to their houses . . . . The sight of the flames served only to increase their exasperation . . . . A poisoned arrow struck the Captain in the leg, who ordered a retreat in slow and regular order; but the majority of our men took flight precipitately so that only seven or eight remained about the Captain . . . . They renewed their attack with fury . . . . As they knew our Captain they chiefly aimed at him, so that his helmet was twice struck from his head. Still he did not give himself up to despair, and we continued in a very small number fighting by his side.

During this battle (picture 54) Magellan was killed when one native thrust a lance through the bars of his helmet, which so weakened him that he was unable to withstand a rush by a large

INSVLA MATHAN.

Victoria

number of natives who hacked him to death. 'Thus', wrote the chronicler when he had reached the safety of the ships again, 'perished our guide, our light and our support.'

THE MOLUCCAS

A new commander, Barbosa, was chosen to lead the expedition, which was further reduced in strength when the King of Cebu turned against the newcomers and captured 25 of them. The Spanish set fire to the *Concepcion*, because they had too few sailors to work three ships. The remaining two ships sailed to the island of Mindanao (picture 53) and Palawan, where they picked up fresh supplies — pigs, goats, fowls, yams and bananas, coconuts, sugar cane and a root which resembled a turnip.

They reached Borneo and visited the king, Raja Siripada, in his capital of Bruni and then on 6 November finally reached the long-sought Moluccas:

On Wednesday 6th November, we discovered four rather high islands 14 leagues to the east. The native pilot told us that these were the Moluccas for which we gave thanks to God and fired all our cannon to comfort ourselves. It need not cause wonder that we were so happy as we had spent 27 months less 2 days searching for them.

Friday 8th November, three hours before sunset, we entered a port on the island of Tidore. Next day, the King of the island approached the ships in his boat so we showed him respect by meeting him. His name is Rajah Manzor. He promised to give us cloves and become a subject of King Charles.

On Tuesday 12th November, the King had a house built in the city for our merchandise. We carried all that we had to barter there and trading began at once.

54 A contemporary drawing intended to show Magellan's countrymen the battle in which he was killed.

THE SPICE TRADE

The Spanish expedition had succeeded in reaching the Spice Islands and in getting permission to found a trading post on the island of Tidore. Their success was sealed by a royal proclamation, in which Rajah Manzor ordered his people to sell cloves to the newcomers. 'All that and the following day we bought cloves like mad.' The Spaniards filled the holds of their two ships with as much valuable spice as they could take, and then prepared to sail home. Fifty-four of the men decided that they would prefer to remain behind. They could not face the prospect of going through the sufferings they had endured on the long voyage out. The rest of the men divided into two crews. The *Trinidad* set off across the Pacific where it was captured by a Portuguese fleet which had been sent to arrest the Spaniards, who had broken the Pope's ruling on the division of the world (page 37). The *Victoria* sailed across the Indian Ocean and rounded the Cape of Good Hope, where its crew experienced the sort of weather that had persuaded Diaz to call it the Cape of Storms. They were nine weeks off the Cape, battling with westerly and north-westerly gales. Once again, the crew suffered from a shortage of food: 'We had nothing but rice and water to eat and drink, all our meat having rotted.'

On 9 July they put into one of the Cape Verde Islands, which belonged to the Portuguese enemy. The boatload of 13 men who had been sent to get fresh food was captured by the Portuguese. The *Victoria* sailed on until, on 6 September 1522, it reached the Bay of Lucar, from which Magellan had set out with five ships and 237 men. The *Victoria*, with only 18 sick men on board, was all that remained of the original expedition. It is not surprising that it was 50 years before another sailor ventured into the Pacific. Then it was an Englishman, Francis Drake, who circumnavigated the world (see *Explorers from Britain*). It is also not surprising that the Portuguese and Spaniards did not try to develop this new, costly, long and dangerous route to the Spice Islands. The route around the Cape was shorter and cheaper.

THE YOUNG HISTORIAN

1 On your map of the world mark the route taken by the *Victoria*.
2 Write the headlines which might have appeared above reports about:
   (a) The capture of the control of the Straits of Malacca;
   (b) Magellan's departure from the Bay of Lucar;
   (c) The entry into the Pacific;
   (d) The death of Magellan;
   (e) The discovery of the Moluccas;
   (f) The return of the expedition.
3 Write short playlets on:
   (a) Magellan and Faleiro (page 63) and the possibility of there being a route around the southern tip of America;
   (b) Preparing the expedition;
   (c) Exploring the Straits;
   (d) The voyage through the Pacific;
   (e) Meeting the natives of the Philippines.
4 Write the letters which might have been sent by:
   (a) Magellan after his voyages up the River Plate;
   (b) One of the crew after meeting the Patagonians;
   (c) Magellan after the return of the *San Antonio*;
   (d) One of the crew on the journey through the Pacific;
   (e) One of the men who stayed behind in the Spice Islands.
5 Make your own illustrations to go with the titles: (a) Through the Straits with Magellan; (b) Our Departure from the Spice Islands.

FURTHER HELP

Books
Groh, Lynn, *Ferdinand Magellan* (Muller)
Wymer, N., *Great Explorers* (Oxford University Press)

Filmstrip
Seawards to India (Visual Publications)